Absolutely Impossible

ISBN: 978-1-365-02467-2

Printed in the United States by Lulu Press, Inc.

Cover art by Kristopher MacGregor.

First Published in 2016
Vancouver, British Columbia

Absolutely Impossible

AN AUTOBIOGRAPHY BY

LORRI MACGREGOR

*Dedicated to my beloved husband, Keith, our children,
and long time friends, Linda, Trudy, and Wendy.*

*With special thanks to our volunteers over the years,
especially Roger, for his inspiration and help with the manuscript.*

Introduction

WORLD WAR II was raging overseas. A baby's cry broke the silence on remote Manitoulin Island, Ontario. The midwife announced, "You have a second daughter". It was decided that her name would be "Lorraine". Little did they know that it meant "Warrior of the Camp". She was to live up to her name.

Lorri attended thirteen schools in three different Provinces as the family moved with her father's job. Her life was filled with academics, music, sports, and dancing.

Grade twelve was marked by a significant life-changing event. Her beloved Grandmother had passed away and she struggled with her grief, wondering if there was an afterlife. Where was God? Who was God? Then she was caught up in a school shooting and her badminton partner died at her feet. Post-traumatic stress set in, but little was known about the condition at that time. No treatment was available. She was struggling to function normally.

In this state the cults came calling, and she was vulnerable. Jehovah's Witnesses took over her life, and took advantage of her desire to know and serve God. She was instructed to cancel her university application, break up with her steady boyfriend, and get married to a Jehovah's Witness. Her obedience to the cult nearly took her life as she refused a blood transfusion, and had an out-of-body experience. It took seven years for her blood readings to return to normal. Pain and illness were her constant companions as she worked to provide for her sons and a non-supporting husband. After thirteen years she broke free from her husband, obtaining a mental cruelty divorce with permission from the Jehovah's Witness elders, provided she did not remarry. Fearing the ongoing retribution from her angry ex-husband, she moved to the relative safety of Nelson, BC. His threats continued.

Perhaps most remarkably of all, GOD sent a man (Keith) into these insufferable circumstances. The rest of the story involved threats, guns, alcohol, break-and-entry, multiple court appearances, politics, barricades, crooked lawyers and the Women's Liberation Movement. Every other moment was filled with searching for truth in the Bible. Out of this whirlwind of activities several life-changing decisions were made.

Keith proved his faithfulness and staying power despite the crushing events. He patiently stood by Lorri, finally leading her to a dramatic born again experience. She truly was converted because she saw Christ in Keith. He proved that not all men were like the JW elders. After their friendship blossomed into love, they married on the JW date for Armageddon, October 4, 1975. Their first desire was to serve the Lord, however there were many barriers.

Ministry was absolutely impossible for this divorced, and remarried couple by man's rules. God, however, opened seemingly shut doors on four continents spanning over three decades. Come along on their incredible journey! You will see what is "Absolutely Impossible".

"But He (Jesus) said "The things that are impossible with people are possible with God". (Luke 18:27).

Chapter One

MANITOULIN ISLAND | I took my first breath in a small Canadian farmhouse on Manitoulin Island, in Lake Huron in Ontario, Canada. A local relative and midwife, who was part of the "black stocking" cult delivered me. I was the second daughter born to Bill and Mary Robison, while the Second World War was raging. My Father could not serve actively as he had no vision in one eye, due to a childhood accident. Instead, he was away at a prisoner of war camp in Northern Ontario, working in the office, and had left my Mother and older sister, Louise, with his relatives on the Island. My Mom was totally out of her element, having been a farm girl from Saskatchewan, before falling in love with my Father in Nelson, B.C., and thereafter following him about Canada, with us two girls in tow.

After the War, Mom took us girls and we lived with her relatives, who were farmers in Saskatchewan, while Dad went on to Vancouver, BC, to get a job and find us a place to live. Mom's relatives had been Dawn Bible Students (early Jehovah's witnesses), but were still being shunned because my grandfather had planted his crops in the Spring of 1925. Armageddon, the end of the world, had been prophesied by the Watchtower Organization to occur in October of 1925. Faithful followers saw no need to plant crops they would not harvest, but my practical family had ten kids to feed, so the seeding and harvesting went ahead. They were disfellowshipped and shunned. When that false prophecy failed, there were no apologies from the local group or the headquarters, and my mother's side of the family were mostly bitter and hostile to religion after that time. One cousin and her family remain Jehovah's witnesses to this day, and still avoid us.

My mother, sister, and myself joined Dad as soon as we could, and settled down to life in a drafty old Victorian house near Kitsilano Beach, in Vancouver, BC. I began kindergarten at Henry Hudson School and could already read and write, since Mother taught me. I could recite from memory every nursery rhyme we had. School required little effort on my part, from that day on, and I always learned easily.

THE INTRUDER | One night when my Dad was away, Mother as usual, had the three of us sleeping in their big bed. My sister always slept at the foot of the bed, while I was beside Mom. I was three years old and my sister five. A burglar broke in and ended up straddling Mom and choking her, demanding money. She woke my sister by pinching her with her toes, and then yelling "police!" My Sister ran down the stairs for the phone, but the line had been cut. I woke up, and when I saw the stranger, my Mother reported that my screaming was so loud and ongoing that the stranger fled the premises! He passed my sister at the foot of the stairs at a dead run and never was caught, nor did he realize any stolen goods. The police were called and a neighbor took us all in for the remainder of the night.

What glorious days of freedom we enjoyed as children in those days-- free to walk to school and home, free to hang out at the beach, free to be carefree children. Dad was often away for his job, leaving Mom and us two girls on our own. Mom took a job at a local restaurant, so often my sister and I were "latchkey" kids after school. It would be unthinkable these days to leave such young children on their own. My sister resented having to "watch" me, so often left me alone. I remember one particularly frightening time when she locked me under the porch with the cobwebs and spiders. To this day that trapped feeling comes back if I go into crawl spaces!

Mother was still deeply influenced by the Watchtower Society and took us girls to meetings and assemblies when Dad was away. I remember being tired from walking long distances and hungry from sitting for hours at these boring gatherings. Once, when alone back at home, I remember blundering into some kind of Neighborhood Bible Camp gathering. I was taken by the arm and told I needed to recite a memory verse. I took the piece of paper and quickly memorized it and recited it, and received some kind of food reward. I left again without being noticed! My one early brush with Christianity! Too bad I was lost in the crowd.

We lived not far from a Sikh Temple, and one day they were having a festival. My little girlfriend and I joined them. We were conspicuously white of course, in a sea of darker skins, plus she had a head of blond curls, and blue eyes. We went up to the ice cream stall and were given a cone each by a smiling attendant. He stamped our hands to show that we had received one. We gobbled down our ice cream, rushed home and scrubbed the ink stamp off and returned to the same stall. We were nervy enough to do this three times, and each time the smiling attendant pretended he did not recognize us. To this day, I smile in remembrance of these friendly folks.

When I questioned my Mother about the different skin colors I saw in Vancouver, she told me a story. We were all created by God from clay. Then He put us in His oven to bake. Some got overdone, some were just right--a lovely golden color, and some of us were under-baked and had white skin. Not only was there no prejudice ever displayed in our home, but I felt others looked better than myself.

We began to move regularly as Dad travelled with the field offices of construction companies and the pipeline installation, across Canada. Mom could have stayed home and seldom seen him, but she chose to follow him everywhere she could. We lived in every kind of rental accommodation, from motels to houses, and we girls changed schools often. By the time I graduated high school, I had been in thirteen schools in three Provinces. This unusual upbringing made me conquer my fears and face new situations, and learn how to adapt to circumstances. Traveling and moving over the years did not frighten me, but helped me face what God had in store for me in later years. When Dad was home we went camping, hunting, and fishing regularly. Love of nature and the outdoors remains with me to this day.

THE PROMPTING | At about eight years of age I felt a strong connection with God, although I had no religious training at home. I was a latch-key child, left alone at home until my parents returned from work. My sister was elsewhere most of the time so I was left on my own. We had a radio and I listened to the "Back to the Bible" broadcast in Alberta. Although the memory did not return until many years later, God showed me that I had knelt before the radio and repeated the sinner's prayer and received Christ as my Savior at that time. I always felt that I was God's child, different from my family.

Desiring to be close to God I went regularly to church with my little Catholic friend, and waited for her in the entry while she went to confession, midweek. I would peek through the door of the sanctuary and the statues and wonder what went on. Priests, nuns, and other people went in and out by me, but never stopped. Another friend allowed me to accompany her and her family to the Church of the Nazarene each Sunday and my memories of Sunday School were stories told by the teacher, but the hunger in my heart to really learn about God went unsatisfied. I wanted to go to their weekly family Bible study, but was told by her Father that it was family time only.

Death nearly claimed me at age eight when my appendix was bursting as they removed it. We had no money for doctors, and no health insurance, so Mother treated my rigid abdomen by rubbing it with camphor ointment and putting a hot water bottle on it. Finally, I clung to her and begged her not to leave me and go to work. She became frightened and called for the doctor. He came to the house, rolled me up in a blanket and ran to the neighbors who were backing up out of their driveway and told them to get me to emergency, which they did.

The blotched incision went diagonally across my abdomen, cutting my muscles, resulting in lifelong pain from scar tissue which formed throughout my abdomen. These adhesions interfered with digestion, ovulation, and childbirth. I was so traumatized by the hospital, the needles, and a burned child in the next bed screaming and moaning, that I begged to go home. Mother took me out of the hospital and I recovered at home eventually, although the incision, done with metal clamps, partially opened and was infected. I also had a polio attack, at age twelve, but survived without permanent paralysis. I also survived bronchitis, pneumonia, and constant colds. I was not considered a healthy child. I was small, but wiry, and excelled at sports.

My sister and I have many memories of being left alone at young ages, sometimes for days, while Mom went away with Dad. My sister was often very unkind to me when our folks were gone. It seemed she could hardly walk past me without punching me. She was simply too young to be left in charge, and took her anger out on me. We enjoy a great relationship today, but it was a long time coming!

My family were mystified as to why I was so drawn to religion, but allowed me to have my way. As mentioned previously, my Mother's family had been bitterly disappointed by the early Jehovah's Witnesses in 1925. To date the Jehovah's witnesses have falsely prophesied the end of the world for 1874, 1879, 1914, 1915, 1918, 1925, the 1940's, 1975, and the year 2,000. Still, they had a hold on my Mother despite their "mistakes". Never did I hear them called what they were, false prophets!

My Father's family were Scottish Presbyterians and regular church attenders until my Grandmother showed up with several pregnant, unwed teenage girls she had taken into her home before the days of welfare. They had been thrown out on the street. The Pastor was outraged that she would bring such ones into the house of God. So Grandmother said if they were not welcome, then her family was not welcome either, and the entire family never returned to church. Bad feelings against religion marked the whole family's history, especially my Father. This attitude colored my upbringing, but I nevertheless prayed to God each night by myself, and so I continued growing up. As we moved often, all church contact was brief or nonexistent for me.

At age twelve I became acutely aware that my Father spent more money than he earned, and my Mother was often in tears, as he spent the grocery money entertaining his friends, driving a big car, and buying expensive clothes. Mom scrimped and saved every way she could, and our diet included a lot of homemade soup and bread, lots of vegetables from Mom's garden, and cheap cuts of meat or no meat at all. She did her best under difficult circumstances, but gave in to my Dad's bad habits and never took a stand. She fit the description of "doormat wife", never criticizing.

Mother was a talented seamstress and earned a few dollars to help out. At twelve, when I could babysit, I told Mom and Dad that from here on, I would buy all my own clothes, schoolbooks, sports fees etc. and all I expected was room and board until I finished school. I kept my vow, always paying my own way. Later on, I worked part time at Eaton's Department Store. I was hired on at the going rate, 85 cents an hour, a big upgrade from the 25 cents an hour I earned babysitting, rising to 50 cents an hour after midnight.

Chapter Two

THE DANCE | By age thirteen I threw myself into my favorite activity, dancing. I was an original "rocker", and loved rock and roll music and Elvis Presley. As I was small, I was a perfect candidate for flying through the air, propelled by my friend's older brother. When we danced, everyone watched. Those were the days of poodle skirts, crinolines, bobby socks and saddle shoes, and good, clean, innocent fun. It was a great time to be alive.

Through the high school years, I was a popular girl, participating in sports, singing in the glee club, cheerleading, and winning an academic award. I had a boyfriend in University, and I myself was filling out enrollment papers for University as an Honors English and Latin major.

TERROR | However, my sweet life was about to be rocked! Change came rapidly. One fateful day before graduation, my friend and I were about to walk into an area where a gunman was about to start shooting. It was our regular route, but for some unknown reason, I grabbed her hand and ran the other direction and out the back of the "wing" of the school. We proceeded outside in the cold weather and entered the other wing where our lockers were located. As I gathered up my books and headed for the front of the school and the exit door, I became aware of a big commotion. I heard several gunshots, unbelievable at that time, especially in Canada. It was March 16, 1959.

Kids were shouting and subduing a gunman, and running towards me I saw my badminton team partner clutching his chest. He fell at my feet and I knelt over him. He tried so hard to talk to me, but no words would come out. I could see a small bullet hole on his shirt front, but hardly any blood. I was frozen on the spot. I was dimly aware that teachers in the office were shouting and crying. Finally, a student who had broken free of the group, stepped over my friend's legs and into the phone booth. I heard him say "Do you still pay $10 for the best news story of the week? There's a guy here who's been shot and I think he is dying". The radio station called an ambulance.

The ambulance attendants picked me up and had to straighten out my arms and legs as I was frozen in trauma. They checked me out for wounds, and when they determined I was uninjured, they took me to the front door of the school and pushed me out, saying "Go home". I don't know how I got home. I lay on my bed and pulled the covers over my head. The phone kept ringing. I was in shock.

Later, my friend died, the only son of a widowed mother. He was so young, only 14, but a big strapping boy. One of the older girls on our badminton team had been flirting with him and had made her dropout boyfriend jealous. He came to our school with the express intent to kill the young boy, and he did. Several students received minor injuries during the shooting, and there were bullet holes in some of the lockers.

For about two years after, I could not watch a shooting scene on TV or movies, where the victim fell clutching his chest. I would run out of the room. I know now I had post-traumatic stress but little was known about it at that time. Two significant events had occurred fairly close together.

MOURNING BREAKS | My beloved Grandmother on my Mother's side had passed away. My Mom and Dad had driven in winter from Edmonton, Alberta to Saskatoon, Saskatchewan to her bedside. She seemed to rally, and even told my Mom that there was a cloud above her bed and she could see her mother and father, and a childhood friend and others, all waiting to welcome her. For this reason, I believe I will see my beloved Grandmother in heaven some day. Perhaps she had been a Christian before getting involved with the Watchtower Society.

It was so sad when I received a call while Mom and Dad were traveling home that Grandma had died. Mom was so excited to tell me that Grandma was getting better, when I had to tell her that she had died. We were all grieving, Mom and Dad and my sister, without benefit of faith. I was still deeply affected by the death of my Grandma, when traumatized from the shooting. I was crying out to God with my questions. Where are the dead? Is there really a heaven and hell? How can I know you, God, when I don't understand the Trinity? I had read in an encyclopedia under "God", that Christians believe in one God manifested in Three Persons. I couldn't comprehend this at all. I determined to accelerate my search for God, to fill the emptiness in my heart.

THE SEEKER | Two churches were within walking distance so I went. The first Priest heard my questions, and then inquired whether my parents were members of the parish. I said "no", and he replied that he was sorry but all his time was taken up by his own parish members and showed me the door.

I proceeded to the next church and asked my heartfelt questions. The Pastor replied that the Trinity was a mystery, and unless I could accept it by faith, then I really wasn't called by God. How could I get this faith? I was told that if I was one of the chosen ones, I would have this faith already. I left confused and unsatisfied, and rejected.

The Mormon missionaries came to our door. They tried their best to go through their chart presentation but my persistent questions about God finally got them to stop and answer me. They told me God was an exalted man who lived on a distant planet with many wives and children. They told me I had been one of these spirit-children before I was born on earth. One of them assured me, that although I had green eyes and brown hair, I still came from a fairly high ranking celestial wife. The blue eyes and blond haired children were usually born into Mormon families. I may have been seeking God earnestly, but even I recognized a fairy tale when I heard one! I sent them away.

Next to arrive were the Jehovah's Witnesses. They were pleasant and friendly and I told them I had many questions about God. They invited me to get my Bible. I remember blowing the dust off Grandma's very old Bible and bringing it into the living room.

A LAMB LED TO THE SLAUGHTER! | Talk about young and naive! In answer to my questions about God, the Jehovah's witnesses always had a scripture when they replied. I did not know Christian doctrine, had no church background, and no one shared salvation with me. Pretty soon they switched out Grandma's Bible (The King James version) for their own New World Translation Bible, which has distorted or removed references to the Deity of Christ. Due to my emotional vulnerability I was an easy target.

Using their altered bible, they soon convinced me that the Trinity was a doctrine of the Devil. Jehovah was God's name, and if I wanted salvation, I had to work for it by obeying Jehovah's Organization. The Bible was used (abused) for all these points. They took me to the Kingdom Hall and I was "love-bombed" and made a fuss over by one and all. Soon, I was "out in service" door-to-door earning my salvation, trying to survive Armageddon by good works, always with fear as my partner.

Looking back, I was so vulnerable and still in post-traumatic stress. My Mother secretly encouraged me, since she still believed in Jehovah's Organization, even though she never attended a meeting. My Father was disgusted with me for "only the weak-minded need religion". With much heartache I gave up my steady boyfriend whom I truly loved, because he would not accept "the truth". He ridiculed and insulted me, alternating with pleading with me to forsake Jehovah's Witnesses. If only he had presented good, biblical reasons, perhaps my involvement would have stopped at that time. I had been pre-programmed by the JW's to expect opposition and persecution.

Why did I do all this at barely eighteen years of age? I did it because I wanted to serve God, I loved God, and I wanted to do His Will. People do not go into cult groups because they want to be weird, they want to serve God! When the genuine gospel is not presented, they are left with a counterfeit gospel and a counterfeit Jesus.

URGENT DOCTRINES | At this time in the Watchtower Society, there was a push to marry young. The hierarchy felt that it was a "protection" from immoral behavior. I attended many JW weddings of sixteen-year-old girls to eighteen-year-old boys. As expected, many of these early marriages ended badly, with everyone being wounded, especially the children. Part of this teaching was that if you wanted children, you better have them now, before Armageddon as the Society was growing so fast. The New Earth might be full with survivors, If so, there would be no need to procreate in the New Earth.

Back in the 1920's the opposite was taught and members were encouraged to be childless and devote themselves to the Organization as there was plenty of time for children in the New Earth! I saw so many pathetic old JW's who gave up having families, and were now alone and ignored because they lacked the strength to go door-to-door or attend meetings. If you can't work, you have no value in this works-oriented organization.

I was taken aside by the JW. Elders and it was pointed out to me that I was getting too old not to be married. My heart still ached for my ex-boyfriend and I had no desire to be married. I was told there were many fine young men in the Organization who had expressed an interest in me, and I should just choose one, and the sooner the better!

The elders pointed out that in Bible times, the parents chose the mates for their daughters, but since my parents were unbelievers, they were giving me this chance to have some say in the matter. I wanted to run away, but felt I had to put God first, before my feelings. Looking back, I was so pathetic and vulnerable, and the elders were so controlling. I couldn't seem to think clearly in my unhappiness.

Pressured, I finally chose Stan, who looked to be an up-and-coming young Magazine and Territory Servant, active in the Organization, but who also shared my love of the outdoors, camping, fishing, and hunting. He had a steady job, and seemed to be a hard worker. All our friends were already married, as I was eighteen and he was twenty-four. We got engaged and the elders were pleased, my family far less so. My consolation was that I was pleasing God and Armageddon would soon be here, perhaps before the wedding!

Sadly, I cancelled my enrollment in University as higher education was frowned on, and "of no value this close to Armageddon", and "just took time away from Jehovah's Service". I entered Business College instead, completing an eight-month course in three months. I was baptized into Jehovah's Organization. The door to a normal life slammed shut.

In the interim before the wedding, I felt a growing sense of dread. Many times I had to choke back feelings of running away from everything. All these events added to my trauma, which was still with me. I had a feeling of "going through the motions" in my day-to-day life of being "normal", at all costs. My ex-boyfriend returned from time-to-time to beg me to leave the JW's so we could have a life. I felt I had to put God first, and went through with the wedding, so I could leave my old life behind and dedicate my new one to Jehovah, as the elders had decreed.

I soon found out what being a woman in the Watchtower was all about. All women were under the authority of all men, especially their husbands. I knew within one month of my wedding that I had made the biggest mistake of my life. I was married to a tyrant, who was also a religious phony. I was nineteen years old and totally trapped. I said "goodbye" to my teen years, feeling that my life was over.

Chapter Three

PRISON | My life became a blur of working, attending five meetings a week on three different days, and going door-to-door with canned presentations like a robot. Every morning I got up to my usual refrain, "He that endures to the end is the one who will be saved" (Matt. 24:13)), or, "Work out your own salvation with fear and trembling" (Phil. 2:12), two out-of-context scriptures that were my byline for survival.

I discovered that when Stan went out in service, the great majority of the time he simply went out for coffee, but counted time for that. Also, his study of the Watchtower consisted of opening the magazine and randomly underlining much of it, giving the impression that he had "studied". He was "Dr. Jeckyl and Mr. Hyde", acting one way in front of others for show, but being totally the opposite at home. He was critical and negative about almost everything and I was miserable from his ongoing verbal abuse.

He ran a thriving moonshine business among the JW's, along with his "purple gas" business. He and his cronies spent a lot of time in our garage, drinking alcohol for which they had paid no taxes, and filling their cars with gas for which they had paid no taxes. Purple gas was only to be used for farm vehicles off road, but Stan forged farm papers to buy it. I knew that I could stop my protests that this was not "paying to Caesar, what is Caesar's, (Luke. 20:22-25) as Christians were supposed to do, when the Circuit Overseer condoned him. I was told that the government was under Satan's control so forget it! Stan financed his private fun activities with his money, but sadly none of it went to household expenses.

Finally, Stan quit his job and failed in an attempt to partner with another man in an electrical business. He just could not be trusted to show up on time or do his fair share of the work. He was a bright man, a gifted electrician, and could weld and do engine work, but only when he felt like it. If I had not worked and paid the mortgage and expenses we would have ended up on Welfare, which he wanted to do, and nagged me about it for years. I steadfastly refused, despite my limited strength to defy him.

A Jehovah's Witness wife is considered the property of her husband, and so I increasingly became an object of his verbal abuse. He had no insight into his failings but he constantly blamed others. He was rude, inconsiderate, and demanding in the bedroom, where his needs were taken care of without tenderness or words of affection. I felt used and abused, and often in pain. I came to hate the JW phrase, "pay your marriage dues", but I complied to "please Jehovah.' I hated my life, and longed to escape.

THE UNSPEAKABLE | Finally, I felt I could take it no longer and moved out into an apartment. I had a good job and continued to pay his mortgage plus all my expenses. Stan went to the elders and cried and "repented", promised to get a job, and begged me to return. The elders pointed out that I had no grounds for divorce and I was to give him another chance, or I would be disfellowshipped for disobedience. It's really a Good Old Boys Club in the Watchtower. I returned, defeated, and with a heavy heart, determined to "endure to the end" as Armageddon was expected any day now. My steadfast love for God held me prisoner in this authoritarian cult.

By this time, I was 23, and didn't want to go through my life without children, so I reasoned that at least I would have someone to love. I quickly became pregnant and was violently ill for the first five months. By the time I stopped throwing up, I was so skinny and dehydrated that my hip bones stuck out. In an attempt to control my vomiting, I was given thalidomide, which thankfully, I threw up! By the time I was full term, I measured only 32 inches around the biggest part of my "bump", and could still wear pencil-slim skirts with only a safety pin enlarging the waistline.

The scar tissue from my blotched appendix operation prevented a normal expansion and I was in constant discomfort and back pain. The worst was yet to come. When labor started and I went to the hospital about midnight, they tried to redirect me to Women's Surgery, since the nurse didn't believe I was pregnant!

I was examined and pressured to sign a release for a blood transfusion. JW's are programmed (with out-of-context scriptures) to refuse blood transfusions. Therefore, the doctors would not perform a Caesarean Section, which I needed, due to pelvic disproportion. My Doctor, (trained in Austria), decided on a procedure not used in North America, which forces the pelvic bones apart and the head is pulled. It was a horrible ordeal without anesthetic, and required 23 stitches to repair the cutting and tearing. I began to hemorrhage while the doctor was attempting to sew me up. I lost so much blood that they could not staunch the flow, and I saw the cleaning staff sopping up my blood with mops and wringing it out in pails! How would I survive this?

OUT-OF-BODY | I felt my life going out of me with each new rush of blood, when I had a strange experience. Although I never lost consciousness, I was aware that the "real me" was standing over by the door, watching the proceedings. Years later I recognized this experience while I was reading literature on torture. Apparently the body will only withstand so much pain and then puts the person into a state where they feel like bystanders--aware, but no longer participants in the pain.

When I tried to share this experience with the JW elders they said it was "not of God". However, I believe today that God spared my life. I was given two quarts of fluid (not blood) and was advised that I could never survive childbirth again. On no account was I to attempt to nurse my baby due to my very low blood count. I was determined to nurse my baby son, at least for a little while. Again, I believe God stepped in, and I had plenty of mother's milk, and my little boy thrived.

Significant time passed after the birth before they had me cleaned up and sewed up and the bleeding stopped. I was told I was lucky to be alive. "Your husband will be happy to see you alive", they said, and sent for him.

Stan came into my room, and without so much as a greeting, launched into all his complaints: "the chairs were so uncomfortable, there was nowhere to sleep, a man shared the room and smoked a cigar. He had had a horrible night!" Since there was no inquiry for my well being, I did not tell him at that time of my ordeal. Why bother? He did say it was a good thing he had a son, as a "man wants a son".

JOY | My young son was a difficult baby, always active, seldom napped for long, and never slept through the night until he was three. At nine months of age, he could not only walk, but run, usually with me in hot pursuit! I loved him fiercely and was so glad to have him. My Mother's love knew no bounds and filled the emptiness in my heart.

I was seriously anemic but could not tolerate B-12 shots or iron pills. My blood count was dangerously low. After nine difficult months, I was pregnant again. I was happy to have another child, even though exhaustion was my constant companion. My doctor told me my pregnancy had to be terminated as I was too ill to survive another pregnancy and birth.

In the 1960's, a woman had to go before a committee of three doctors to authorize a termination of pregnancy and the mother's life had to be in danger. My doctor had it all arranged for me to appear and then immediately have an abortion. Here I was, a traumatized young woman in poor health, but I stood up for life and would not agree. The difficult pregnancy continued to term, with similar experiences to the first one.

The delivery was again difficult but at least my second-born was in a proper birth position. His older brother was born upside down with his arm coming first. By the time my second son was born he looked like he had been in a battle. For both boys I was so dehydrated from vomiting that I carried no water. Randy was covered with a stubborn sticky mucus and his head was elongated. Bright blue eyes looked into mine as he raised his head, and I knew he was okay despite his troubles. There was no hemorrhage, thankfully, but again, many stitches were required due to tearing.

The last two hours before his birth were traumatic. They could find no heartbeat for him and I heard the nurses whispering that he would probably be stillborn. It is almost unheard of that his heart was obviously beating, but in sync with mine. Truly a child of my heart. He was born with health issues due to my ill health throughout the pregnancy. He had eye damage and poor lungs, but his brain was fully functional. We both lived, proving the doctors wrong. We were far from well, but both alive!

He was so different from his brother. He napped willingly, slept through the night after a few months, and was an incurable cuddler. Health issues were always there, particularly his asthma, and we spent many nights in the rocking chair when he was ill. When he was older he would say, "You sleep, Mom, I can rock myself". All my love and devotion went to my beloved boys, and I truly was a "smother mother".

When Randy was six weeks of age, I was still in major discomfort due to the tearing, and very swollen and sore, still requiring a rubber cushion to sit. My husband announced that he expected his "marital dues", and with no regard to my protests, proceeded to take them. I could hardly breathe for the pain and ended up being sent to the hospital for surgery and repairs. My doctor was so angry, and I believe he let Stan know what he thought of him! Thankfully, he never again acted with such brutal force.

After this surgery, the staff could not wake me up from the anesthetic. Finally, they pulled the curtains around my bed and left me. My Mother, who had come to care for the boys was frantic because she could not come to me. Stan had taken the opportunity to go away hunting and did not bother to check in with my Mother. He also told my her he was going to one area, but went to another. The police (RCMP) even looked for him to try and get him to my bedside, but he could not be found.

Finally, I regained consciousness. It took me a few moments to realize I was in a hospital bed. There was a woman with her head down across my legs sobbing her eyes out. I was puzzling over this when she looked up and saw that I was awake. That brought many more tears. Finally, when she could talk, she told me she had recently lost her daughter in a similar situation to mine, and was grieving at my bedside. She was an off duty nurse. She alerted the staff and I quickly began to recover. Soon I was able to take my shaky self home. My Mother stayed on to care for the boys and I. I believe now that God spared my life, for the ministry that was to come later.

ZOMBIE YEARS | So, life went on. I refer to these years as my "zombie years". My blood did not come back to "normal" for several years but began to improve when I got some organic iron tonic and felt much better as my blood count went up slowly. I was determined not to let my health rule my life, so forced myself to go out in the door-to-door service and to the meetings. I also conducted a "bible" (book) study with a lovely older woman, and with my own boys. I also had to go back to work part time to pay the bills. We lived on the edge of poverty, as Stan's income from illegal sales of moonshine and purple gas went for his own pursuits of hunting and fishing trips, and not for family expenses.

My Mother's training on how to economize was so helpful as I bought only basics, made everything from scratch, and held on. Of course, Stan provided wild meat from his hunting and my beloved Mother-in-law raised chickens for us, so all that helped. I was reported for going into the Salvation Army Thrift store for clothing, and was reprimanded by the elders for "supporting a false religious organization". What a judgmental, unloving organization! Where would they suggest I shopped, with an income lower than the poverty level!

Chapter Four

LIGHT | My Mom and Dad had just retired at this time and had bought a lovely beachfront property near Balfour, B.C. The highway ran through the property and there were two lots above their homesite. They gave a lot to my sister and one to myself. I longed to take my boys near their grandparents, but how was I going to afford it? I knew my part time wages from typing invoices and clerking at Sears was not going to do it. As I grew stronger physically, my old independent nature began to arise. I determined that I was going to take my boys and escape from Stan, if he would not agree to go, and be decent about it.

I knew commission sales were the only way I could earn enough to leave, and build a small house on my lot in BC. I signed on with the company who had provided my organic iron tonic. They also sold a line of organic cosmetics (not available in stores then), and a revolutionary bra design not available in stores. Stan was unreliable as a baby sitter so I befriended a young girl, twelve years old, from across the street to help me. At first, she cared for the boys so I could have a bath, and then learned to give the boys their bath and put them to bed. She would stay with them until Stan came home for the evening (out of the garage). She was a treasure!

I not only booked "parties" (similar to Tupperware), but quickly proved myself a saleswoman. I guess I should thank the JW's, because if you can learn to sell their magazines door to door, you can talk people into anything! I also recruited other women to be representatives, so got an overriding commission on their sales. Soon, my little escape hoard began to grow. I became a District Director in the company, and earned even more. I worked hard, and most importantly, was there for my boys. They would only be without me for an hour or so in the evenings, so didn't get a chance to be a lonely kid like I was. They adored their babysitter also. Hope rose in my heart.

All this was in addition to being a JW in good standing. I wrote to the Society asking if the area I had my lot in was a "go to where the need is greater" area. They wrote back encouraging me to make the move, as workers were needed in that area. I had carefully priced out everything needed to build a modest A-frame house. My Father, who had built his own cabin, was willing to help me if I could just get there somehow.

I had one funny instance in my novice plans to build. I was pricing out trusses for the roof and called a company I found in the yellow pages. I inquired about the cost of the trusses I needed, when the man said, "just tell me where the hernia is!" There were not many laughs those days, but this was one.

GRASPING FOR FREEDOM | Finally I was ready to go. I confronted Stan and told him I was leaving, with or without him. He could either co-operate with the move and remain with the family, or be left behind. I told him if he came with us, he had to find a job and support the family. He had to be a better father, and JW. He tried to get the elders (his garage drinking buddies) to order me to stay, but I played my trump card-- my letter from Watchtower headquarters. They didn't dare advise against that! He decided to come.

To Stan's credit, once he knew how serious I was, he helped out by building a box on his hunting truck to move our "stuff". We made several trips back and forth. He even found an old "bunkhouse" which we fixed up to live in. Talk about rustic! We had no running water, no electricity, and cooking and heat were a wood stove. There was an old fruit shed on the property to hold his junk, and we camped in the bunkhouse while we began construction on the house. I had arrived!

My Mom and Dad were on the job immediately, with my Father taking the lead and Stan reluctantly complying. The nearby hunting and fishing were a constant temptation and he managed to make the acquaintance of several other laz-abouts who rarely worked and lived on the dole. They were the bane of my life! Mom, Dad, and I carried on as best we could. When the house was ready for wiring we thought Stan would step up and do his job. He was a licensed electrician, after all.

It ended up we three attached the boxes and the breaker box, drilled holes in the studs, pulled all the wire through and all Stan did was hook up the wires at each end. Never mind! We had electricity at last, which made life much easier. Stan did fence the property with barbed wire and his brother gave us a dairy cow, which Stan milked. We raised a pig, and had chickens. We finally moved in to the semi-finished house.

I sold milk, cream, and eggs to give me a cash flow of $10 per week. With that I bought the basics, flour, salt, sugar, etc. Everything else came off the land. With Mom and Dad's help, I grew a large garden which provided vegetables which lasted all year. Each Fall I bought potatoes, onions, cabbage enough to last through the Winter, which kept quite well under the house. I picked and stored boxes of good cooking apples from our old orchard. I made bread, butter, and cottage cheese. We had little cash flow, but lots of good food to eat. Now it was time for me to provide an income for the family again, since the odd jobs Stan did gave him income for his chosen pursuits. Reminding him of his promises to provide for his family did not work.

While the boys were pre-school age I ran a daycare out of my home. I completed the course from the government first, and for several years cared for two babies, four preschool children, and two after school children. It was exhausting, as I was not completely well yet, but I would not leave my boys. My memories of being a latch-key child coming home to an empty home fueled my determination.

Finally, the boys were both in the local school at Balfour and I was able to seek a better job. I became the Office Manager of a small Nelson Estate Planning business, which also sold insurance. I loved the job and my financial situation improved. The only draw back was the twenty-mile drive to work and back on a winding, often treacherous road. Stan seemed to become even more unreliable as I needed him more to help out at home. Often the boys came home to an empty house as he was off with his friends. This angered me and brought back unhappy memories of my lonely childhood.

Also, Stan's behavior was worsening. He had always been verbally abusive, but now he often physically punished the boys excessively for no good reason, or he allowed bad behavior without consequences, depending on his mood. I wanted him to go for mental help but the JW elders take a dim view of their members seeking help for mental problems. The JW's seem to think that going out in door-to-door service and attending all meetings solves all behavior problems. I could not overcome the advice from the elders, nor could I control his bad buddies. I was miserable and trapped, but determined to change things.

Often, I would return home tired, to find that Stan had not put the dinner I left for the family on to heat. The table would be littered with dishes from the all-day coffee break he and his friends had engaged in when I was gone, and no chores done at all. The house reeked of cigarette smoke, dangerous for my asthmatic son. If I criticized in any way, I was subjected to a barrage of verbal abuse in front of my boys. Pleading with the JW elders for help did no good at all. It really is a man's world in the Organization, and women are encouraged to shut up and put up. After all, Armageddon was only "months away".

Chapter Five

THE STRAW THAT BROKE THE CAMEL'S BACK | I had "endured to the end" as the JW elders encouraged me to do for seven long years in Balfour, and six long years in Edmonton. An incident pushed me beyond all endurance that September. Several JW families from Edmonton had taken to parking their RV's on our acreage for their vacation. Some of them were people that could not have been bothered to drive across Edmonton to visit us, but word had spread of our free parking and use of our house in a vacation wonderland. Stan invited them in to use our washer and dryer, washrooms, and use produce from my garden. My expenses for utilities went up alarmingly, along with my grocery bill!

I came home that long weekend in September to find that our JW visitors had taken everything from my garden, at Stan's invitation to "help themselves". I had planned to lay away my winter's supply of vegetables in the freezer as I did each year, but they were gone! The visitors had used my laundry baskets and thoughtfully left the dirt in them for me to clean. Those who had not left yet, were sitting in my living room waiting for me to prepare something to eat. Freeloaders! Greedy grabbers! I lost it! I turned into a screaming banshee.

I threw them all out and told them to get off my land immediately and never come back. Then I took Stan's clothes and threw them out the window into the yard and told him to leave and never come back. He went, smiling smugly, because he knew the JW elders would order me to take him back. They tried, but I would have none of it. They threatened me with death at Armageddon, for disobedience, but at that point, I preferred death. I was well and truly finished with Stan, no matter what!

The next business day I went to a lawyer and filed for a mental cruelty divorce. I changed my locks and began my new life as a single Mother raising two boys. I asked Jehovah God for His mercy, and the elders granted me permission to be a single Mom. I knew I was not free to remarry or date, but I was free! I hired a neighbor to come and be with my boys after school. I never felt loneliness, only relief. I honestly didn't know why any woman would want to have anything to do with any man, at any time, for any purpose, any way! I continued to be a faithful JW, enjoyed my job and my new life with my boys. I felt Jehovah had been merciful to me and I was still a faithful JW, and Armageddon was still "months away".

The only problem was the round trip to work when the roads were so treacherous during the winter, or hopelessly clogged with tourists in the Summer when the ferry let the traffic off. One day my car went into a dangerous skid on glare ice. I came very close to going over the embankment into the glacier-fed lake but at the last possible moment spun in the other direction and ended up in the ditch next to the mountain. As I sat there shaken, but unhurt, I knew the time had come to move into Nelson. I had to be safe and available to care for my boys.

I prepared to start my new life in a new location, and to rent out my Balfour house. Stan continued to harass me and I felt isolated and unsafe in my remote location in the country. Property prices were low at that time, and I had managed to save a small down payment. With my job, I qualified for a mortgage. My house hunt in Nelson began.

Chapter Six

FREEDOM | I was free to find a new home where my boys and I could feel safe. Being a single Mom with responsibilities was nothing new to me. For the last thirteen years I had carried the financial and religious load. I had filed for a mental cruelty divorce. The elders at the Kingdom Hall had given me permission since they, too, were sick of false promises and outright lies from Stan. They finally gave me scriptural grounds and their approval to be a single Mom.

2 Thessalonians 3:10, says "... if anyone is not willing to work, then he is not to eat either". Verse 14 continues, "If anyone does not obey our instruction in this letter, take special note of that person and do not associate with him, so that he will be put to shame". This fit Stan, so I was granted freedom after thirteen years of bondage.

In my house hunt, I was partial to the old Victorian houses in our heritage town, but knew I had to be wary of things like no insulation, old wiring, single windows etc. In those days before home inspectors, I needed to find someone who could help me.

One day a man, Keith MacGregor, walked into our office, and to my surprise, into my life. He was a land developer who had bought a parcel of land next door to my boss' business partner. His marriage had failed, and he had come to Nelson to start a new life. He inquired about me and was told that I was a "man-hater", and did not date but lived like a hermit with my two sons, and it would be best if he just avoided me.

This was true. I could not imagine what any woman would want with any man at any time for any reason. Period. I was not lonely, did not crave companionship, and lived a quiet life. Silence was preferable to the verbal abuse I had endured for years.

I was a Jehovah's Witness in good standing and attended all meetings required of me, and engaged in field service, door to door, meeting all quotas. I knew it was a short time till Armageddon, due in October of 1975. This was 1974. I was content to be alone, and serve Jehovah God and wait for the new earth. My friends were all JW's, except for the friendships extended to me at the office.

The fact that my marriage had ended without adultery being committed by either party meant that I could not remarry unless Stan committed adultery. The committee of elders at the Kingdom Hall advised me of this. This suited me fine. I knew remarriage was not in my future! As it happened, Stan did go out and commit adultery, but I didn't care. I continued in good standing with the JW's.

I had found a great old Victorian house hanging off the side of a hill. I loved it, but knew I had to be careful. This was before the days of home inspections. I made inquiries for a contractor to check it out, but couldn't seem to find one. Paul, my boss' business partner, took it on himself to ask Keith to help me, as Keith had constructed many homes in the Okanagan. He came to talk to me. I was wary.

Keith is a very soft-spoken man with a gentle manner, and offered to check out the house for me at no charge. All he asked was that I have dinner with him first, as he had recently moved to Nelson and didn't know many people, and was tired of eating alone. I told him I did not date, but I would have dinner with him so that he could check out the house I found. The price was right!

What a strange first meal! I watched him across the table with suspicious eyes, for any indication that he might make advances towards me, but there were none. I relaxed a bit. We went off to inspect the house. Keith found inadequate wiring, dry rot, and windows that all needed replacing. The furnace barely worked, it was so old! He told me the "fixes" were more than the selling price, and strongly advised against buying it. I was grateful for his help. I reluctantly gave up trying to go "Victorian".

Finally, I found a house that he approved. It would require a few minor fixes, but was structurally sound. Keith had taken to dropping by the office at lunchtime and hanging around me, and since he was just friendly, I didn't send him away. We ended up sharing lunches on a semi-regular basis and our friendship grew.

I closed the deal on the house and began my move to town. Every day I loaded my car with all it would carry and unloaded before returning home.

Keith came by and offered to let me use his Van to go back and forth to town, and he would make do with my car. I was suspicious of his motives but very glad to have the Van, which quickened the move considerably. He was "killing me with kindness", and my opinion of men certainly didn't apply to Keith. Finally, I was in my new home and the renters were ready to move into my house at Balfour, in the country. I was optimistic for the first time in fourteen years.

Chapter Seven

ERUPTION! | All hell broke loose! Stan broke into the Balfour house, changed the locks, and barricaded himself in with a good supply of rifles and ammunition and plenty of booze. He had been making moonshine for years and had plenty to drink. He had also hired a lawyer, Mickey Moran, known for his devious, clever tactics who was interested in setting a precedent case in Canada, and making a name for himself.

Under Canadian law, a wife who had stayed home, could now sue the ex-husband for half the proceeds of the house upon death or divorce, even if the house was in her husband's name only. My case was the opposite. I had been the sole breadwinner, and had built a house with proceeds earned only by me, on land that had been a gift to me from my parents. The Women's liberation movement was in full swing, and Mr. Moran hoped to take advantage of it, by securing half ownership for my stay-at-home husband, who had contributed nothing.

Stan also decided to get serious with Jehovah's Witnesses since it was just a matter of months till Armageddon, and the JW elders assured him that, as a woman I could not truly own anything. Since the husband "owned the wife" in their reasoning, and the grounds for my divorce were "unscriptural", he had every right to take my home as his own. Also they told him, the father had greater rights to the minor children, and he needed to get custody away from me. Otherwise he would be "blood guilty" when his children died at Armageddon with me, should I persist in my "independent" behavior. His JW support team was considerable.

FAMILY INJUSTICE | I was then told by the elders that since Stan had "repented", I needed to return to him immediately and submit to his leadership. I had been through this scenario several times before, recognized the phony repentance, complete with tears and promises, and knew what returning would mean--more abuse. I begged Jehovah to have mercy on me, but I could not repeat the mistakes of the past. For the first time in fifteen years, I refused to obey the elders. Instead of remaining as before, I was actually out of my abusive marriage, and I knew I would never return.

The elders gave me stern warnings, but as I had such a good record of service to their organization, they said I could remain a JW, but they were watching me! This was the first time in 15 years I had refused to obey them immediately. I had equated obeying the elders with obeying God, but now I was not so sure the elders were obeying God.

FRACTURED AUTHORITY | I was forced to hire a lawyer to answer the child custody matter. I was falsely charged with being an unfit mother. The JW's knew very well that Stan had never been a proper father or husband, yet they knew I was defying them, so threw their support behind Stan and his false charges. It is truly a man's world in the Watchtower! Every time we went to court, his lawyer entered a "stay order" and put off the hearing. This happened some fourteen times! Every time cost me more money I didn't have, since I no longer had rental income. It was a ploy to break me and impose their will on me once again.

POISON PROPAGANDA | There was one kidnapping attempt at this time. I had spoken to the school principal and the teachers at my boys' school. I knew that children were often kidnapped by the non-custodial JW parent and spirited away, usually across the border. This was prior to passports etc. that protect children now. There they would be placed with a strong JW family, who undertook their upbringing in the Organization. All the JW's were comfortable with lying to authorities, as Armageddon was near, and they were "saving" these kids through Armageddon. This doctrine is called "justified lying".

The children, including mine, were told that Jehovah hated their custodial parent, and that parent would die shortly, at Armageddon for disobedience. They were told they needed to love Jehovah above all else, and be faithful to these new arrangements, and then they would be reunited with their non-custodial parent and live happily in Jehovah's new earth.

Thankfully, God protected my children, and before they were driven off from the playground at recess, the principal went to the vehicle and opened the door and told my boys to get out and return to the school grounds. The vehicle roared off. We all looked out for the boys 24/7 after that, but the strain was nearly unbearable.

FAITHFUL | Through all this Keith stood by me. I had informed him some time back that if he wished to see me, outside the office setting, the only thing I would do is study the Bible with him, nothing more. To my utter surprise, I heard a knock on my door one evening, and there stood Keith with the biggest bible I had ever seen. "Well Lorri," he said, "I'm here to study the Bible". I was flabbergasted!

On the one hand, I had said this to send him away. On the other hand, I could "count time" having a study with him, much easier than going door-to-door when I was so upset over the children and my rental house. I opened all my curtains on the kitchen windows surrounding the table, turned on all the lights, and invited him to sit down at the table. I wanted to keep him in full view from the alley at all times, so I could not be accused of entertaining a man in my home.

I had come to trust Keith enough that he could be in my home in the presence of my sons. We began a weekly bible study that somehow happened even more often as Keith would show up with his bible, and often brought treats I could not afford, like fried chicken and pizza. My boys loved to see him come, complete with his Great Dane giant dog who was good natured like his owner, and it was good to see my boys laughing. Even my cat liked Keith and the dog! Keith also began doing acts of kindness, like reattaching my sagging drainpipes, fixing my sink, and other odd jobs.

LOOKING INTO THE WORD OF LIFE | Our "study" progressed along. Looking back on it, it was hilarious. I could pound him into the ground with selected scriptures. He admitted that he was so biblically illiterate that he had to look in the index to find the New Testament. He had snuck into the local Christian bookstore and got "Kingdom of the Cults" by the late Walter Martin and secretly prepared himself.

He shared with me how, as a young man, he had gone forward at a Billy Graham Crusade in Toronto and given his heart to the Lord. He told me he knew he was born again, and even though he had failed many times, Christ had never left him nor forsaken him. He knew he was "saved" and going to heaven. That's all he knew!

GLOW | "How dare you be saved?!" I cried, "I've done good works for fifteen years, and I don't know that I'm saved!" We went round and round, until one day Keith came and I knew something was different about him. He seemed to be radiating inner strength and resolve about his faith! I was puzzled. He had some kind of inner "glow".

Turns out he was so frustrated with trying to reach me, he had fallen to his knees one night and earnestly cried out to God to help him reach me. As he knelt there, he felt the presence of God fall on him and he began praying in an unknown tongue. He had no idea what had happened, but he felt strengthened to try again with me. He somehow knew not to tell me about this. As a JW I would have thought he had a demonic encounter!

He challenged me with new boldness, along with his gentleness and radiating the love of Christ to me. He challenged me to prove from the Bible that Jesus Christ was Michael the Archangel, as JW's believe. "No problem" said I. That was until I began my own research in the books of JW's to give Keith scriptural proof. When I finished, I had major problems believing it myself! The doctrine was obviously formed by unrelated fragments of scriptures, linked together without regard for context. I was very upset.

DOCTRINAL DELIBERATION | There are only five scriptures mentioning Michael by name and he is identified as "one of the chief princes" in Daniel. So who were the others? JW's taught that Jesus was unique. Something was wrong. Also in Jude, how come Michael did not dare rebuke Satan, yet Jesus could rebuke Satan? Also, why did the Archangel Michael say, "The Lord (Christ) rebuke you" if Michael was the Lord Jesus Christ! Also, when Christ comes again in the bible account in Thessalonians, "with the voice of the Archangel", does that make Him an archangel? He also comes "with a shout" and "with a trumpet". Did that make him a shout, or a trumpet? I doubted a doctrine of the JW's for the first time. "Was I believing in the wrong Jesus Christ?", I asked myself in anguish over many sleepless nights. I scoured the Greek/English Interlinear Translation and found Jesus Christ referred to as "Ho Theos", yet the Watchtower Society claimed that was a title for "Jehovah", Almighty God only. Could Jesus be God? My head hurt. I was in turmoil.

Chapter Eight

I CONFRONT THE ELDERS | I requested a meeting with the elders at the Kingdom Hall, a most unusual thing for a JW to do, since these meetings are usually for some unpleasant discipline, but I needed answers! I had honest-hearted questions. They were the spiritual leaders.

I began by saying that someone was disturbing my faith and had challenged me to prove from the Bible that Jesus was Michael. I said that I had come to them to get answers for my questions which I then shared. I expected we would have prayer, and then they would straighten me out, and I would leave satisfied with good answers for Keith, from the Bible. My faith as a Jehovah's witness would be restored.

Instead I looked up from my Bible into hostile, angry eyes of three "brothers" who had all been my friends for years. One pounded his bible and said to me, "If the Watchtower Society says Jesus Christ is Michael the Archangel, then he is Michael the Archangel". That settles the matter! Another one asked me how I dared to question Jehovah's Organization. The final one forbid me to ever speak to this person again, and if I did, I would be disfellowshipped for disobedience. I was quickly shown the door. No prayer, no answers, angry responses--I reeled out in disbelief.

BREECH | I remember feeling like I had been kicked in the stomach by a mule! Where was the love of God in all this? I contrasted the cruel elders with gentle Keith. I could see Christ in Keith, not them! Yet I feared being disfellowshipped by them and failing to save my sons through Armageddon! I was so torn, but I told Keith he had to go away on a permanent basis. I was fond of him, but I had to put God first!

I turned to the Bible for comfort, determined to find out who Jesus really is, if He wasn't Michael! I chose the purple "Kingdom Interlinear Translation" published by the Watchtower Society, and read the English words under the Wescott and Hort Greek text. In Colossians 2:8,9. I found out one could be deceived on who Christ is, and not only that, but "...all the fullness of the Godhead (Deity) dwells in Christ, even in the flesh!" On the Watchtower side, I realized they had altered the Greek text, to suit their doctrine, even inserting extra words into the Greek text "translation". I was shocked at their deception with the word of God! More evidence of scripture twisting was right before my eyes, especially concerning the Deity of Jesus Christ. I knew Jesus was probably not Michael, but could He be "God"? My mind was reeling.

Everything was coming down on me at once. My court date had finally been set for the near future. Could it really be that the Watchtower had deceived me, lying about who Jesus really was? Would Christ really come into my heart if I asked him? I could not deny that I saw Christ in Keith. It was all too much. I was desperate!

Late that night I fell to my knees and cried out to God. I was going to say "Jehovah God" to start, but to my surprise I called out "Jesus!" I continued on that I didn't know for sure who He was, but I wanted to know for sure! Was He Michael, Almighty God, "a god"? Only a good man on earth? I knew in my heart that Colossians was correct that there was some kind of mysterious Godhead. Intellectually, I couldn't figure it out, but I ended up crying out "come into my life and into my heart, and show me who You are!"

BIRTH | As I knelt there, I felt what I can only describe as a "cloak of peace" fall upon me, and my whole being was filled with peace in the midst of all my turmoil. Then I felt a warmth in my heart. It felt so good and I knew Jesus had "come into my heart". I stood up a new creature in Christ! Somehow I had called out for Jesus and He had heard me! I had truly been reborn!

The next morning, I called up the head elder and told him to take my name off the membership list. I was no longer a Jehovah's Witness. I still was not sure what the whole truth was, but it wasn't them! From henceforth I would serve the Lord Jesus Christ, and seek His truth in His Word alone. I intended to call Keith to come back, but he showed up of his own accord and upon seeing me asked "Did you pray and receive Jesus Christ as your Savior?" I wouldn't answer him. I don't like admitting error! He was right, and I was wrong.

He went to my record player and put on two LP's he had brought me. One was by Bev Shay from the Billy Graham Crusade and he sang a line, "He's in my heart, I feel Him there". That did it--I said to Keith that, yes, I had prayed and received Christ in my heart, and I had terminated the JW's! He was so happy! Still the court case loomed, which would decide the fate of my rental house, and the custody of my sons.

We ended up knowing all the tactics the enemy lawyer would bring. An office friend who had worked with me previously got a new job as bookkeeper at a local hotel/restaurant. Her assigned desk was against a thin wall and on the other side was a private table in an alcove, where the enemy lawyer met with his cronies and witnesses at the restaurant and discussed my case. We knew I would be a subject for a character assassination, not from anything I had ever done, but from rehearsed false testimonies from Jehovah's Witnesses who were prepared to lie under oath. He felt I had to be proved "unfit" in the matter of child custody. God help me! Obviously placing my friend where she was, showed that God's help had already begun.

I had been such a good JW, that I had virtually no friends outside JW's to testify that I had been a good mother. The friends at the office were willing to be character witnesses for me, but had never seen me in my home with my children, so were not suitable. I went to a few close women friends in the JW's. They turned away with tears in their eyes, telling me the elders had instructed them not to help me, as I had chosen to question Jehovah's Organization. They could be subjects for harsh discipline by the elders for refusing instructions to testify against me. I applaud them! I was driven to constant prayer for God to somehow help me, as I had only my parents and Keith on my side. I soon learned that Jesus Christ and myself were a majority in any situation. What a life lesson! I have never forgotten that one!

Chapter Nine

OUR DAY IN COURT | So, there we were in the historic courthouse in Nelson. A holding room for witnesses was packed with JW's, willing to perjure themselves for the Watchtower Society. There is a doctrine in the JW's called "justified lying", which allows for false testimony, if it benefits the Society. Those JW folks really believed they were saving my children through Armageddon, but none could look me in the eye. Betrayal is a horrible feeling. To their credit, some of my former JW friends refused to join in.

We sat outside the courtroom, waiting for our case to be called. I was so traumatized, I was beyond speech. All I could do was cry out in my spirit, "Jesus! Jesus! Jesus!". Finally, my case was called. At that moment I truly could not bear it any longer. It was all too much; my rental house would be lost; my precious boys were to be taken away; and my piano, which I treasured in my heart, was gone from the house. Stan told me he had sold it.

Still I clung to Jesus. My parents were unbelievers, but Keith's head was bowed in prayer. Their lawyer, who moments before had been marching about with a cocky smile on his arrogant face came up and stood before me. In dread and fear I lifted up my eyes, feeling totally drained. Suddenly, he spun on his heel to face the JW's and to everyone's utter amazement, made this proclamation: "I am not going into court against this woman. She will keep custody of her children". Turning to Stan, he said "and you, Stan, are going to pay child support".

If anyone had a camera handy at that time and panned both sides, the resulting picture could have been entitled "The Village Idiots" as all of us were open-mouthed in amazement, including my lawyer. Still he rallied himself and papers were signed after a short delay, giving me full custody of my sons, including child support (which I never received).

DIVINE JUSTICE | Stan's claims against my house were dismissed and I was free to take it back. I couldn't imagine how to do this, with Stan and his guns keeping me away. Finally, as we left the courthouse I displayed my lack of Christian maturity by going up to the JW false witnesses and saying, with all the contempt I could muster, "You bunch of Judases"! To their credit, they hung their heads, guilty as charged!

Stan came up to me and said, "Lorri, I lied. I did not sell your piano but hid it at the neighbors and I will give it back to you. Call me next week." I borrowed a truck that same day and we rescued my piano. What a God we serve!

I now got the details of how the claims against my house were dismissed. During this time, the Women's Liberation Movement, headed up by a lady who was at the local New Democratic Party Headquarters in Nelson had heard of my dilemma. She lobbied her contacts in the Government then in power in BC. The Attorney General's wife agreed to help, and that same day the local RCMP (Royal Canadian Mounted Police) received instructions to take me to my house, break in, and remove all Stan's weapons and property. The "Stay order" against me was rendered useless, overridden by the Attorney General of the Province.

The Women's Liberation Movement was determined that a single mom, who was the sole support for her family, and the sole owner of the house could not be treated in this manner, by a non-supporting, abusive husband. I am so grateful to them for helping me. Keith came along with me with a new lock and installed it for me. We were so thankful to God for His deliverance from my troubles. I became an absolute believer in Jesus Christ and have trusted God, big time, ever since! My faith rose straight up and never came down. It has stood the test of time. I give God all the praise.

I thought I had lost it all, but in twenty-four hours, Jesus gave it all back to me. I have trusted God for everything ever since. I also trusted a man for the first time in fifteen years, and accepted the idea that there were good men in this world, and Keith was definitely one of them! I allowed my heart to soften at last, and there was no denying his devotion and love for me through all these afflictions. Other women tried to get his attention, but he felt God meant for him to be with me. We have stood the test of time.

Chapter Ten

HEARTS UNITE | Shortly after, Keith was sitting at dinner with us, and I remember looking up at him across the table, and the realization hit me that I loved this man, and wanted to spend the rest of my life with him. That feeling has lasted over forty years! We both know we love and serve the God of the second chance!

GROWTH | The next months in our lives fell into a pattern. Every moment I was not working, I was buried in the Bible. I knew I would never trust anyone ever again to tell me what to believe. I did get a concordance with every word in the Bible in it, and started in looking at every scripture I could find, first on the subject of Jesus (Christ, Messiah, Lord etc.). I had realized that I needed to pray first for the help of the Holy Spirit to guide me, so I spent countless hours straightening out my beliefs, on God, salvation, prophecy etc. I was relentless in my pursuit of truth. Keith got the benefits of Bible truth at last and grew in grace along with me. I was scripturally free to marry Keith by this time, as my ex-husband was committing adultery. Keith was free to remarry as well.

Keith got down on his knees in April of 1975 and asked me to marry him. I told him I could not marry him because my health was not good enough. I had chronic abdominal discomfort from a blotched-up appendix surgery as a child, and a painful scar tissue mass interfered with my digestion and bound my ovaries causing pain and swelling which can only be defined as a chronic "toothache" in my abdomen.

Also, I had been told another pregnancy would end my life. The doctors would not prescribe birth control pills for me due to my history of blood hemorrhaging. Surgery was a major undertaking for me due to the adhesion mass and would risk my life, so that was advised against. I would not inflict myself and my health problems on Keith! I tried to send him away so he could have a better life with a healthy woman.

This should have been enough for any man to get up off his knees and run for the nearest exit, which I expected. Instead these big, strong, arms came around me and as he cradled me he said, "You need taking care of, and I want to take care of you. Please let me". He vowed to love and care for me, no matter my health. I knew by now that God had sent this man to me. I loved him and trusted him, and we vowed to serve the Lord together, and do our best to mend our broken lives. After that our priority was to to nurture our children.

I was 31 at this time, and Keith was 41, so we weren't kids. My boys needed a real father in their lives, and Keith also loved and accepted my boys. They were fond of Keith, too. He knew we came as a "package". We were blissfully ignorant at this time of just how big our "package" would become!

SPECIFIC SYMBOLISM | We decided to marry on the date the Jehovah's Witnesses had set for Armageddon, October 4th, 1975. We knew there was no danger of their prophecy being fulfilled, as they had missed Armageddon a few times before: 1874, 1914, 1915, 1925, the 1940's, so 1975 wouldn't work for them either. Instead of my life ending, it would just be beginning!

My parents hosted our wedding in their Lakeside home, and my relatives that I had virtually ignored the whole time I was a JW, graciously forgave me and came out to support me. My two sons were there, as well as Keith's two sons. His young daughter was still with her mother. The Lutheran Pastor, (who had visited me to offer his prayers and support during my troubles) married us. A kind, concerned man, he was nothing like the rigid Jehovah's Witness elders.

TROUBLE IN PARADISE | We left for our honeymoon in Spokane. It lasted one night and then my Mother called to say she could not handle our combined kids, who were together under one roof for the first time, and determined to act badly. My Mother was a strong woman so I knew things were bad.

Keith and I knew we had to go home and face the music. "Home" was a beautiful new house Keith had built for us all. The rebellious teenager never did go back to his mother, but remained with us. Eventually, Keith's daughter came to stay also. His oldest son also arrived in the area, and soon became a father while very young, so we had this to deal with as well. Still, nothing could drive Keith and I apart. We were then, and still remain a team. We are a threefold cord, not easily broken, as the Lord promised.

Chapter Eleven

ALL IN THE FAMILY | A learning curve remained over the years while the kids were growing up. There were times I felt like running off screaming into the night because of the kids, but never because of Keith. I am sure there were times he felt the same, but because the Lord was with us in our family problems, we persevered. I confess we looked forward to "Empty Nest Syndrome". We did our best to love all our children and treat each one equally. Eventually, we ended up with the five children, (who grew up and produced eight grandchildren, and six great-grand children, and we love and appreciate them all! Our daughters-in-law are the greatest! We were the "Brady Bunch", but we had no "Alice"!

MOULDING | Keith taught me so many things. He taught me to control my temper with our blended family, and would sneak up behind me, kiss me on the neck and say "What's the matter with my Pussycat?! As a result, I could never stay mad for long. He was no push-over, telling me that I was not just my boys' mother, but I was his wife. He would insist we go away to have some alone time. He taught me that physical love between husband and wife was a beautiful thing, that two soul mates could become one in every way. Our bond was so strong, my pain had to fade into the background. My previous view that "paying my marriage dues" was something to be endured became a dim memory. We truly loved God first, and then each other, and then our joint kids. Our home was filled with love. We were overcomers in Christ in an ongoing basis, and we enjoyed our escapades as a blended family. Then we enjoyed our adventures after the formal child-rearing was complete, as well. We still do!

BREAKING FREE | After our marriage, we wanted to give our blended family a strong tradition of going to church. This was a big step for me, as my mind had been poisoned by the JW's against the "corrupt church" and the use of the cross. The first day we entered the Lutheran Church I had to close my eyes and run in the door under the cross. A crowd moved me along a bench and boxed us in. In my angst, I looked up and saw another cross over the altar, but I couldn't get out! I didn't want to shame Keith, so I stayed.

I relaxed when they began to sing the old hymns as the words were so profound. They moved me the same way my Bible research did. I loved the enthusiastic singing, some of it in 4-part harmony. The people were so welcoming, I finally relaxed. Coffee and treats after the service were a nice surprise as refreshments were never served in the JW's. People lingered and visited, another big difference from the Kingdom Hall. We made new friends. I was hooked on church!

THEOLOGY OF FEAR | The Lord taught me other lessons as well, during these years the kids were growing up. The vast majority of JW's know they must go in door-to-door service and work really hard to place magazines and start at least one "bible study" so that they might be saved, maybe, depending on how well they have done to be faithful to the Organization. There was the constant fear present that one had not "done enough", attended enough meetings, placed enough Watchtower literature to be finally saved, when the dreaded Armageddon arrived. Salvation could be yanked away from the JW's, even if they were to survive Armageddon if they are not obedient to the leadership for all eternity. "Forget grace and get to work" was their true motto!

FREEDOM TO LOVE | When I was saved by grace and truly reborn in Christ, I remember reclining in our big easy chair and saying, "Grace, grace, wonderful grace! I never again was compelled to knock on doors or even share my faith. I love this grace!" Trouble was, people kept arriving at our door and would ask questions. I had to respond, I couldn't help myself. People got saved, prayers were answered, and our faith grew. One day when I was in prayer, I felt the Lord saying to me, "You see, Lorri, you tried to convert people by your own efforts for 15 years, but it was a tough job. Aren't things better when they are done by the the Holy Spirit?" Yes! I relaxed and let the Lord bring people across our path. We enjoyed the sharing, and began to see many fruits in our lives. Our happiness grew daily.

ASTONISHING EXPERIENCE | One night I was awake, just silently praising the Lord for His goodness, while Keith slept beside me. Suddenly I felt a rush of incredible peace come over me, and I continued praising the Lord, but this time in an unknown tongue. I woke Keith up and shared what had happened. He told me that the same thing had happened to him when he had prayed alone in his cabin, asking God for help in reaching me for Christ. He confessed he often used this prayer language ever since. I was astonished!

I knew that "tongues" were talked about in the Bible, but was taught that the gift had passed away with the death of the apostles. Furthermore, the Watchtower teaching was that if we ever heard tongues, it was Satanic. I now knew better, and could hardly wait to tell our Pastor. I said to Keith, "The gift of tongues has passed away, but God has given us tongues. I think we're the only two people in the whole world who have this gift today". (1 Corinthians chapters 12 and 14).

COLD WATER | I'll never forget our Pastor's face as we shared our news. It went from concern to shock and disbelief. He stiffly informed us that tongues were from the Devil, and if we wanted to continue in this practice, well, there was a whole church in town who carried on shamelessly with tongues. We more or less got the left foot of fellowship out of the Lutheran Church unless we renounced our experience. We were too busy praising God!

We showed up at the local Pentecostal Church and adapted as best we could. I harbored suspicions that some of the "tongues" were of the flesh and not the Spirit, and we really did not like the loud voices some used. Neither Keith nor I have ever spoken out loud in tongues, but we did pray in the Spirit and sing in the Spirit. We loved the praising of the Lord that went on, and I found great freedom in eventually lifting my hands to God and truly entering into praise and worship of our wonderful Savior.

I was not used to being hugged. Our family did not hug, and a firm handshake with the relatives and friends was the most I was used to. My Mother did hug me as a child, but that became occasional as I grew older. When church people started hugging me I was very uncomfortable and even twitched sometimes. However, eventually I relaxed and even started to hug back! Now I hug all the time!

PABLUM | Every church I went to, I was disappointed in the lack of teaching. Keith called the sermons, "sermonettes for the Christianettes". The Bible study classes were conducted by a person who monotoned through the outline provided. There had been 15 people in attendance for the last 15 years. Boring, boring, boring!

I, on the other hand continued on in my study of the Bible every chance I got, used the scriptures to witness to people, and was in love with God's word. I prepared scripture presentations for the JW's and Mormons, and generally educated myself so I could witness effectively to anyone looking for answers.

We really enjoyed "camp" at the Lake property in the summer. There was a big, old, metal building that kept the rain off, and we really raised the roof praising God. The one sore spot was that some of the Pentecostal women liked to bring up our divorce and remarriage. Some even suggested I leave Keith and break up the family. One lady shared that a "Pentecostal Divorce" might be the best thing and I should sleep on the couch and discontinue marital relations. Such a downer, like dripping water! It troubled me deeply.

One night at camp I stayed behind to seek God about all this. I knelt down on a mat on the concrete floor and began by saying to God that I was not leaving until I had heard from Him. After some time I felt God's Spirit ask me a question. He said, "what did you pray for all those years as a Jehovah's Witness?" I replied that He already knew. I prayed for a good husband, a good father for my children, and a loving lifetime mate, who loved God as much as I did. I again felt the Spirit say, "Yes, I heard that prayer, and behold, now I have given you the desire of your heart". I jumped up off my mat and said aloud, "No one will ever lay condemnation on me over my remarriage ever again". Attempts to do so are dismissed immediately. I have heard from God! "There is now no condemnation for those who are in Christ Jesus". (Romans 8:1)

Chapter Twelve

EARLY EXPERIENCES IN THE MINISTRY | Soon God began a call on my life to teach the Bible. I tried my best to dismiss this as I was a woman first of all. I quoted scriptures (out of context) to God, telling Him I was under His command to be silent in the church, etc. etc. However, the call was like fire in my bones and I finally approached the Pastor about it. The denomination frowned on women teaching mixed audiences (men and women), but he felt I did have a call from God. People we witnessed to were now attending his church. However, the denomination would not allow divorced, remarried people to be on the board or teach at that time. I kept telling God I was a divorced, remarried, WOMAN, so I could never accept His call to teach. "Please God, leave me alone!" I was not left alone, and the call got stronger and stronger.

Finally, the Pastor stepped up and told the board that he was going to start a small, new converts class in the kitchen of the church, around the table there. We had a couple saved out of the Bahai religion that desperately needed teaching, and he was willing for me to teach them. I diligently prepared and prayed. Soon, the couple had told others and we were getting a little crowded in that kitchen.

BREAKING THE RULES | At the time the church was in a building program and the old church got sold. For the interim meetings, the church rented a local community hall. The facilities were not wonderful, but there was a fairly large furnace room and the New Converts class got assigned to the furnace room. The Board was also getting suspicious that so many extra people were turning up but weren't at the approved adult class. They decided to confront the Pastor and myself to verify the rumors, that I, a woman, was teaching, while the Pastor sat there condoning this breaking of the church rules.

I still remember the two militant board members yanking open the furnace room door to confirm their worst fears during the class. There were so many people in attendance, that we were all standing upright as there was no room for chairs. I was teaching from a narrow spot behind the furnace, the only place left to stand, peeking out at my audience. Their jaws dropped, they exchanged a glance of astonishment and shut the door without saying a word. The Pastor and I were in for it, we knew!

TROUBLE AMIDST REVIVAL AND RENEWAL | Sure enough. The cat was out of the bag. At the same time, the Full Gospel Business Men's fellowship got started in Nelson, with Keith as the first president. In those days, it was simply men sharing their heartfelt testimonies of how they came to Christ. It was effective, beyond belief almost. Keith, through the FGBMF, brought twenty families to the Lord and into the Church. Most of them came to my class, rather than the traditional one.

What were the church elders to do with us? Keith and I were faithful workers during the construction, had contributed generously to the building fund, and were certainly an asset to the congregation, although we could not hold office or teach. Still they were happy to get our tithe money, although they had pointed out that we could expect "whatever small measure of grace God saw fit to bestow on us". Period. We would have been treated better if we had been murderers in our former lives, rather than divorced and remarried! We refused to be offended by them, and were determined to serve the Lord however He could use us.

A generous gift we had made to the building fund didn't hurt us either. We had received several thousand dollars unexpectedly from an residual inheritance settlement and gave it all to the church. When the church ran out of money towards the end of the building program, we hired a worker from our small corporation we both owned, and put him to work on the church. Another contractor did the same, and the building was completed.

Both the Pastor and I were awaiting the Board's decision. Since the church was in revival obviously, they were reluctant to offend all the new tithers, and they had hoped the new church would be filled up after all. Finally, one day before the opening of the new church I got a phone call. I was told that I had no standing as a teacher in the church, due to my gender and remarriage, and as such I would not be assigned a room in which to teach my class. I hung up the phone and cried many tears, including crying out to God asking why He had allowed this? I was so upset. My spirit was in turmoil.

That night I hardly slept, and spent most of the night between light sleeping and waking. I had strange dreams, or visions during the night which I did not understand at the time, but were a picture of our future international ministry. As I woke, I heard the words in my spirit, "I will make you the head and not the tail". I thought this was very strange, but Keith and I determined to show up for the adult class and the opening ceremonies for our new church, got up and got the kids ready for church. The phone rang before we left the house.

STUNNING MOVE | One of the Board members, with hardly a greeting, said, "We have assigned you the main sanctuary for your class from now on, so please use it this morning." We were somewhat incredulous but praised the Lord for His faithfulness. I taught that class in the main sanctuary until we left for our new ministry adventures in Vancouver, BC. When I left, the average Sunday attendance in the class was 105. Praise God!

Chapter Thirteen

NELSON | We soon realized that our location nine miles out of Nelson was turning us into a glorified taxi service and way too much valuable time was spent commuting. We decided to move into Nelson to my house there, which was being rented out. We commenced major renovations. Every day we came with our packed lunch and worked until the kids came home from school. We put on an addition to accommodate our larger, blended family.

TRANSPARENT LIVES | It was summer and our windows were open. One day there was a knock on our door and our neighbors stood there. To our surprise, they had come over to see what we were all about. They asked how we managed to work together and not argue and fight? They wanted a strong, compatible marriage, so would we please share our secret for the happiness they had observed? Of course we did, and they were both born again, and are still serving the Lord today! All this because our windows were open!

During these busy years with raising the children together, running our land development business while Keith was overseeing the FGBMF, were very full. As I was preparing and teaching each week, we did one other service for the Lord: we hosted all the speakers who came through the men's fellowship or visited our church. What a blessing! We made friendships that endure to this day and we grew so much in the Lord by ministering to these saints who also had a call on their lives.

In addition, we also invited in whoever came to our door from the Mormons to unsuspecting JW's. Also, many folks came to our home for prayer or counseling. Our children never knew who would be there when they came home from school, but got very used to hearing the Bible discussed, or earnest prayer going on.

One day the Mormons were showing us a video presentation on their church. Our youngest son arrived home from school and sat in on the presentation. As the trumpet was sounded, the slick presentation came to an end with the words, "So, we can see that the Church of Jesus Christ of Latter-day Saints is the only true church on the face of the earth!" Our ten-year old Randy stood up and walked away past us all, shaking his head and proclaiming: "Boy, now I know why Jesus said false prophets would arise and mislead many!" I had to flee to the kitchen and silently laugh as our stunned visitors packed up to leave.

DRAMATIC RESISTANCE | Another church in town sponsored a meeting with an ex-Satanic Priest who claimed conversion to Christ. Other churches were asked to help out, as it was being held in the High School Gymnasium. There was a good crowd, and the speaker was ministering to people in front of the stage. Suddenly the local Witches Coven marched in, formed a circle, lit black candles, and began their Satanic invocations. Everyone froze and they were the center of attention. I ran to the Pastors present to do something. They just stood there. I approached some of the ushers, church leaders in Nelson. They refused to do anything.

I was so indignant and prayed, "Well, Jesus, you and I are a majority in any situation, so let's do something!" I went to their circle and "broke the circle" and stood in their midst. They gasped in shock as the circle "must not be broken" under threat of death or dire circumstances for anyone who would dare do this". I said to them, "You are not welcome here. This is a Christian gathering paid for by Christians. Blow out your candles and leave the building, in Jesus' name!" To everyone's surprise, they blew out their candles and filed out. Thank God for the empowering of the Holy Spirit when needed! The witches waited for a long time in the weeks to come for their curses to land on me because of my humiliation of them. All that fell on me were the Lord's blessing and protection, as promised in the word.

THE AWAKENING | God also blessed us by allowing us to be a part of my parents' salvation. My Mother had been an early Jehovah's Witness, called the "Dawn Bible Students", who met in the local schoolhouse as she was growing up. The end of the world was announced for 1925 and there was great excitement, with Armageddon promised for early October. As soon as my Mom's family planted their crops they were disfellowshipped for being unfaithful. The whole family was shunned, and Mother lost her best school friend, who would no longer speak to her. They all became disillusioned and somewhat bitter over religion. All her life Mother felt the JW's really had the truth, even though they had made a mistake in 1925. She secretly supported me in my life as a Jehovah's Witness and even had a JW bible study with me when father was not around. However, when I became a Christian, Mother could see the difference my rebirth had made, and accepted Jesus Christ as her Savior soon after. We both prayed for my stubborn Father.

Father was steeped in Science Fiction and felt that only weak people needed God. He ridiculed all religion. He had lost an eye in a childhood accident so could not go to war. I was therefore born during the war, while he ran the office for a Prisoner of War camp in Northern Ontario. He brought along my Mother and older sister, leaving us with his relatives on Manitoulin Island in Ontario, a big culture shock for a Saskatchewan farm girl.

BLIND | However, Dad could not deny the change in my life, and he and Mother loved Keith and told anyone who would listen that he was the Son they had always wanted. Keith got Dad to attend a Full Gospel Businessmen's banquet and witnessed to him. Dad was so stubborn and was alone one day, railing against God. During the encounter Dad lost all vision and finally cried out to God in his blindness, a broken man. His vision returned. His conversion was immediate and life-changing. Dad and I forged an incredibly close relationship in the Lord which continued until his death. Keith and I took Mother and Father into our home and lovingly cared for them for ten years. Both went to be with the Lord at age 93.

MIRACLE | Mom, Dad, and I visited Mom's brother, Uncle Jim in the nursing home near the end of his long life. At that time, he was Canada's oldest surviving type 1 diabetic. He was the only one who had remained faithful to the Watchtower Society and was one of the "elite" remnant of the 144,000. We witnessed to him and he accepted the true Jesus Christ and will be with us in heaven. He went to be with his Lord in his nineties. He was a well-to-do bachelor and the Watchtower Society was already counting his money when he changed his Will, leaving them only a modest gift.

LIFE LESSONS | I remember one day when our beloved family cat came home poisoned. The vet told us we should have her put down. The three younger kids living with us at the time begged us to not put the cat down. They asked me to pray with them for the cat's healing. I looked into these three sets of trusting eyes, and could not refuse. Meanwhile our Catholic neighbor had dropped by and was standing at the open door while we prayed.

The neighbor was angry with me and said, "What are you doing to your children's faith? What will happen when that cat dies?". I replied "What will happen if that cat lives?" The cat lived!

At this time, I was also speaking in the surrounding area at churches and other meetings, and helping out ex-JW's who were hurting from being expelled from the Kingdom Hall. We were also urging Christians to invite the JW's and Mormons back, and Keith and I would show up for the visit and they could have a firsthand lesson in witnessing for the Lord. God blessed all these efforts with much fruit, and we continue this practice to this day.

FIRE! | Jesus continued to educate us in how much He loved and cared for us. Every Spring we went to my property in Balfour to burn off the long grass. We had missed the year before, so it was extra long. Big winds often come up in that location. We were as prepared as we could be, with hoses and sacks to beat back the flames but an unexpected big wind whipped up the fire and it raced across our fields. I was on the top of the hill and Keith was below the hill. Both of us were exhausted from trying to beat back the flames to no avail.

I saw the fire heading for the large cedar trees (full of oil) and the neighbor's house on the other side. If Jesus did not intervene the fire could wipe out several houses. There was not even a volunteer fire department at that time. I placed myself between the racing fire and the cedar trees. The flames were waist-high. The cedar branches touched the ground. I cried out to Jesus to help me. The fire came so close to me I had singed eyebrows and eye lashes and a very red face, but I stood my ground. Suddenly the big wind stopped abruptly and a gentle wind from the opposite direction came up the hill and turned the fire back on itself and it burned out quickly. An exhausted Keith came over the hill and said "What happened?" What indeed! What a God we serve!

STOLEN VEHICLE | Another time friends were attending a banquet when they realized their truck had been stolen. We gathered around them and earnestly prayed. I felt led to pray that the thief would just leave the truck "right now", unharmed, and it would be returned to our friends.

We later determined that at that moment we prayed, the thief abandoned the truck in an uninhabited area between Balfour and Kaslo. The police returned the truck but could not find the thief, who had left the keys in the ignition, and the door wide open while he fled. How we all rejoiced and thanked God! We had many more answers to prayer, proving God's goodness over and over.

Chapter Fourteen

ENTERING FULL TIME MINISTRY | Keith and I made plans to travel to the Full Gospel Businessmen's Conference in Phoenix, Arizona early in 1979, and Mother and Dad were anxious to come as well. We made arrangements for the kids' care and set off on our trek. The Pastor and two other couples completed the convoy. We travelled together to Los Angeles. Our Pastor had leanings towards the Word Faith Movement, and wanted us all to go there first. He and the two other couples were enthralled with it, but Keith and I came away feeling it was unbalanced teaching. They remained in the Los Angeles area and my parents and Keith and I travelled on to Phoenix. Both Keith and I felt that God was calling us into full time ministry, but we frankly did not understand how He expected us to do it!

After all, we both had a divorce and remarriage, and I was a WOMAN with a calling to teach! Not allowed! Keith emphatically said he had no calling to teach, but felt called to help me any way he could. God had already intervened to allow me to teach locally, but we both knew something else was in the future, but HOW!? We were soon to find out!

We had no tickets to attend the Full Gospel Businessmen's banquet in Phoenix, but Nelson friends of my parents were able to secure four last minute seats. Mom and Dad sat with their friends, and Keith and I took our two tickets and sat with strangers. My table companion was a Mexican evangelist, full of enthusiasm, as wide as he was tall! The noise level was so great that one could only speak to the person beside them. He said he needed help as the JW's were attracting even Christians from his home town in Mexico. Could I help?

All I had at this stage were legal-sized sheets of paper I had typed out from my search for the true Jesus Christ vs. the Watchtower Jesus (Michael the Archangel), with the appropriate scriptures. I said I would get him some copies as I had made some to bring with us. I also felt led to give him a gift of money for his humble outreach.

Just before intermission and the offering, my new Mexican friend passed out one of his testimony books to each couple at the table as a gift. He had been in a street gang, involved in drugs and violence before his conversion to Christ. Now he was a street preacher, living by faith. He got up and left the table. I went out during intermission and saw him at his table in the lobby, selling his books. I went over to give him our offering to help his ministry, and told him I would go out to our Van and bring back the papers I promised him.

As I was walking away with my purse over my arm he called out to me and said "give me your purse". He seemed surprised and said "I don't know why I said that". I said, I don't know why you said it either, but here is my purse. Now, those who know me know I would never do this, but I did, and that act saved all our money, travelers' cheques, and credit cards! I took my keys and left the hotel. Our van was parked a few feet from the door under a bright light and I had no hesitation in walking over and opening the side door.

SIGNATURE EVENT: BANG! | Suddenly I was pushed into the van by a black man who held a gun to my head. I sat down in the driver's seat sideways, facing him. I have never felt fear like that in my life. He said "I'd just as soon kill you as look at you--give me your money!" I sank down into a puddle of fear, drowning in it. Suddenly a scripture rose up in me, "God has not given to us a spirit of fear, but of power, love, and a sound mind". (2 Tim. 1:7) I felt strength rise in me as the next scripture hit: "All things work together for good for those who love the Lord and are called according to His purpose".(Rom. 8:28) I responded by saying in my mind, then I will not fear in Jesus' name. Knowing the call on my life from God, I added, "Jesus, if You can call me, then You can keep me".

I raised my head to this young man and an amazing thing happened, I felt nothing but pure love for him, and I felt the Holy Spirit fill the Van, like a cloud in the temple must have. He felt it too. He tried to recover his "tough-guy self" but it was hard with me smiling my "Jesus loves you" smile right in his face. I told him that if he needed money he didn't have to steal it from me, I would give it to him in Jesus' name. All he had to do was come back into the hotel and let me get my purse. I told him how Jesus changed my life and could change his too. I found out later that I was gone 20 minutes, but I had no awareness of the passing of time.

Twice the gunman told me to get on the bed we had in the Van, but I just ignored him and kept talking. I did tell the Lord that I would rather join Him in heaven than be raped. Still I felt no fear, only incredible love as I shared.

Finally a yellow car filled with other young men pulled alongside and began shouting "What are you doing?" "What's taking so long?" The gunman became very agitated, waving his gun at me and grabbing what he could. He took my parents' leather jackets and our small TV and began backing out the side door of the Van. He leveled the gun at me and said "I'm sorry Lady, I didn't want to hurt you". He fired the gun and I knew I could not survive at about three feet from me, point blank range. The acrid smell of the gunshot went up my nose. I clutched my midsection and thought, "at least I'll die with the name of Jesus on my lips". I began to cry out "Jesus, Jesus, Jesus...". After about twenty-six cries I realized I was not dead yet-- probably only wounded. I began feeling my midsection for the wound and couldn't find one. Incredulous, I jumped to my feet and cried out "Hallelujah, he fired a blank!"

I found out later, that had he fired a blank, I would have been wounded at that range. I was still in possession of my diamond rings and gold watch, and my purse was safe, thanks to my Mexican friend, who kept it under his book table. Thank God the robber had not taken my precious notes! I got them out to take in to my Mexican friend, and headed back for the hotel.

As I walked in, Pedro came running up to me and said, "Are you okay? What took you so long?" I said, "Oh, Pedro, I was mugged in the parking lot". This was overheard by Hotel Security and they rushed up to me and told me not to move until the Sheriffs arrived. Pedro went and got Keith who was still busy talking and thought I had gone to the washroom. He rushed out to me.

The Sheriffs came, tall, lanky, with pistols strapped on--(right out of Hollywood, I thought! They took Keith and I to an interrogation room and asked me to tell them everything that happened. I said "Everything?" "Yes", they said. They had their writing pads open, but soon their pencils stayed suspended as I shared it all. We went outside to the Van, and they found a smashed up bullet which was laying under the rug at my feet. They couldn't find a ricochet anywhere and there was nothing between the gun and myself to divert a bullet. They were clearly puzzled.

My description of the gunman and his friends led them to believe that they were the same gang of hoodlums that were then operating in the Phoenix area. Other victims had been taken in their own vehicles out to the desert, robbed, raped, and shot dead. Why did they not follow their usual pattern? Why indeed?

As the sheriffs walked away, one turned to the other and said, "This whole evening has been very strange".

PUBLICITY | We went back inside to the conference, which was now over. The editor of the Full Gospel Businessmen's "Voice" Magazine rushed up to me to interview me for a story. Only one other lady had ever been the topic of an article in that international magazine, and that was the Founder, Demos Shakarian's wife! I shared that I was from a small Canadian City, Nelson, B.C. and that I had once been a Jehovah's Witness and was now dedicating my life to reaching them for Christ, and teaching Christians how to do so. Then the article went on to relay the shooting story.

Upon hearing what happened, my Mother exclaimed, "Take up the large shield of faith, with which you will be able to extinguish all the fiery missiles of the evil one!". (Eph. 6:6). We drove back to their friends' place and tried to settle down for the night. I removed my ankle-length dress and Keith held it up to the light. There were five bullet holes though the skirt, and one bullet hole through my slip. The dress was of flimsy fabric and was bunched up behind my legs as I sat facing the gunman. I began to shake as I came down off my spiritual "high" adrenalin rush, and realized how close I had come to death. I did not want to talk about the experience to anyone, other than to the Lord, as the shock set in. I recognized post-traumatic feelings (PTSD) again in my life.

As we drove back to meet up with our Nelson friends, I prayed as we drove along, and the Lord reconfirmed our ministry call, and also showed me that the supernatural love I felt for that unlovely gunman was how He looked at people. I have never forgotten that lesson, and do my best to look at all people as the Lord looks at them, with love and compassion. Still, I felt the trauma and needed to be left alone.

AFTERMATH | We had arranged to meet our Nelson friends at a buffet in Las Vegas. I cautioned Keith and my Mom and Dad not to say anything.

Our friends were already at a table waiting for us. I let Mom, Dad and Keith take the trays to the table and I was last, to pay for the meals.

The cashier was obviously an aging showgirl. She had gobs of makeup, including false eyelashes, and a very low cut outfit. As I was paying, she said, where have you come from? I said "a conference in Phoenix". "What kind of a conference, she said". I was desperate to leave, and not talk to anyone, so said "a religious conference". "Oh", she said, "I've been thinking about religion lately. I wonder if God would care about me, given my past".

Well, that did it. I couldn't walk away. I took my small bible out of my purse and went through the salvation message briefly with her. The lineup was getting longer but she said, "You mean grace is free and Jesus Christ will forgive me and I can be saved?" I said "Yes!". She said I'm getting myself a Bible and I'm going to pray as soon as I get off shift to become a Christian". Black tears from her false eyelashes loaded with mascara were streaming down her face and dripping off her chin, but she didn't care--God loved her!

Those at the table were laughing at me. "Look at Lorri! Now she's got her Bible out and is preaching to that woman!" The Pastor was still shaking his head when I sat down to my cold food. God had just snapped me out of my trauma and I shared about the shooting with everyone, giving God the glory.

I haven't stopped talking since!

FLOODLIGHTS | God was not finished. When the *Voice* Magazine hit the worldwide distribution, letters flowed in from all over the world, and we had to go to the local newspaper to have thousands of copies made of my notes. Everyone who wrote thanked God for sparing my life, but needed information and help with the Jehovah's Witnesses. We were invited on national TV on 100 Huntley Street in Toronto (seven appearances in all), and trained their counsellors. We also shared several times on "It's a New Day" out of Winnipeg, Manitoba. Churches from all over invited us to speak. God was launching our ministry! Never mind that we were divorced, remarried, and from an obscure location in Canada. God opened doors that no man could close.

One day, after the magazine was out, I received a phone call. "This is Bill Cetnar, calling from Kunkletown, Pennsylvania, and we're going to start a conference for ex-Jehovah's Witnesses to get together and share how they came to Christ. I thought it was a crank call from a fictional place-- Kunkletown indeed! However, it was real and turned out to be a very special destination for a lifetime. We met others like ourselves for the first time. We had all been "lone rangers" and were novices in this type of ministry. Over the years, we formed many lifelong friendships and helped many people. We treasure our memories from the Retreat to this day. We missed some, but kept up our attendance for over two decades. The outreach continues to this day.

CONNECTION | Back in Nelson, at our local church opening, Pastor Bernice Gerard was the speaker. We were very drawn to each other from the first, recognizing a like spirit in the Lord, and a willingness to serve Him. She invited us to come and speak in Fraserview Assembly in East Vancouver at our first opportunity. As our ministry blossomed, God blessed us by having my parents participate in that ministry by moving into our home and taking over the household and the children while Keith and I travelled. The kids were all thoroughly spoiled by Grandma and loved it when we left and Grandma came.

On our first trip to Fraserview Assembly with Bernice Gerard, when I got up to speak for the first time, I felt the Holy Spirit speak to my spirit that this was to be our home church. Keith felt the same way. We returned to Nelson and made plans to move to Vancouver.

Chapter Fifteen

METROPHALIS | We planned to sell our house, but again God intervened. American Christian friends phoned us and said they were praying for a family in dire straits who had been ordered to leave the country until their immigration papers could be straightened out. They were from Malta, had two children, and were in ministry. As the group prayed, our names popped into their heads, so they phoned. We needed rent money at the least to help pay our expenses in Vancouver. They promised to pay rent, if enough money came in from their supporters in the USA, but if not, they still needed shelter. We let them move in in faith, and our rent was paid each month! Amazing God!

So, our house couldn't be sold. We tried to sell two lots we had on the market, but they didn't sell either. We were "property-rich" but cash poor. We still had our good credit rating, so we took a demand loan and purchased a fixer-upper near Fraserview Church in East Vancouver. At first the interest only payments were manageable, but then interest rates started to skyrocket, rising to 18%. We were determined not to use money from the ministry for our own use. All income went into outreach and to pay our ministry travel expenses. We served as volunteers for over thirty years in this manner. We never made an appeal for money, but God met our every need.

Finances were very tight when we moved in faith to be on the Ministry Team at Fraserview. My budget for food was $50 per week, and we had three bottomless-pit teenagers in a growth spurt, plus our older son who often stopped by to eat. We found we could buy reject potatoes for $2 for fifty pounds from a local market in Richmond, and bargain vegetables, and made do with those. I baked my own bread and made soup and everything else from scratch. Snacks were popcorn and bulk cereal. It was a good thing I was raised by a "depression mother" who knew how to economize. Then we received word the family of four from our rental home in Nelson were coming to stay with us for a week to straighten out their immigration papers. Double mouths to feed! I took my $50 to the local discount market and prayed I could manage.

Asking the Lord's help I entered the store. As I went along the meat counter, the butcher came out and marked down a large package of ground beef. He continued on to two roasts, and some stew meat. I rounded things out with chicken. I needed some extras as well and my cart was full when I got to the check-out. I held my breath as items were rung up. It was a long tape and the clerk said, "something's got to be wrong with this." "How much is it, I asked with a tremble in my voice?" "$49.99" she said. I left the store with my penny, rejoicing in the Lord and I never did add up the tape! God had once again provided.

Our ministry continued in Vancouver and was very fruitful and blessed. We helped Pastor Bernice Gerard launch Sunday Line on TV, and I appeared as a regular guest each week, as well as running the make-up department. We were on the church ministry team through the expansion of the church and its resulting frustrations. We often did late-night radio programs for Sunday Line and also radio programs on KARI radio. We often had only one night a week where we were not booked in one outreach or another. We were exhausted.

We were relieved to finally resign from the church team as our ministry had grown so much we could not do both. We continued our close relationship with Bernice Gerard, and Sunday Line. She shared many confidences with me, which I have kept even after her death.

INTERCONTINENTAL | We were invited to minister in Australia by the Assemblies of God, who arranged our first 60 day tour. We were to return in the future, with a 90 day tour, and then one for 120 days. I spoke 120 times during the 90-day tour from one end of the country to the other. What adventures! We premiered the Godmakers movie and the Witnesses of Jehovah movie during our tours. The films remained behind to continue to bless Australia.

FILMS | Now to some background on the Mormon movie. God used us to bring that documentary about, in a round about way. God had put on our hearts to do a documentary exposing the Jehovah's Witnesses and the Watchtower Society. We shared our vision at the Blue Mountain Retreat during an ex-JW conference. This was before the days of digital cameras and a 16 millimeter film would cost the film partners $250,000 US to complete . A former JW elder shared our vision, and set up a corporation to raise funds. Many joined in with shares of $5,000 each.

We knew of one multi-millionaire Christian businessman in Vancouver, BC who had helped fund a film called "The Cult Explosion" with Jeremiah Films. He had been a Mormon at one time before his conversion to Christianity, so Keith and I invited him to Fraserview Assembly to hear our friend, Ed Decker (a former Mormon) speak. We approached our rich businessman about helping to fund our documentary exposing the JW's. He was very interested.

However, Ed Decker thought there should also be such a film about the Mormons and he solicited our funding right out from under us to produce "The Godmakers". Our dream was not dead yet, as our multi-millionaire friend promised to help fund our JW film when he had recouped some of his investment from the Mormon film. He was eventually as good as his word. Meanwhile, the rest of us were buying shares in the proposed "Witnesses of Jehovah" film. We joined in the research and script planning.

ENTERPRISE | Keith and I had been volunteers in the ministry for some years and money was tight. We determined to raise $25,000 towards the cost of the JW film, so we returned to the business world briefly to do so, while continuing the ministry. We borrowed money from the bank and bought one of the few remaining acreages on Kootenay Lake. We put a road in and subdivided the larger parcel into lots to sell. The profits from the larger parcel would give us $25,000 profit to donate for the film, which we did, gladly.

BLESSINGS DELAYED | That left an adjoining small parcel of land, once a dock for the paddle wheelers that travelled the Lake, in earlier times. It had a nice beach on a quiet bay and I was determined to buy it so we could spend our retirement years enjoying it. It lay unused for over twenty years, as the ministry carried on. Now, however it has become our very special retreat where we enjoy our Summers, since we are (semi) retired. It is a very special place to us, and we consider it God's gift to us, as we could never afford it at today's prices. God is good.

A few years ago, we thought we had lost our beach paradise. There was an extensive flood on Kootenay Lake and many folks lost their sandy beaches and were left with a pile of rocks instead. Most of our living area was under water so we took a trip away, waiting for the water to go down. We returned to our lot with anxious hearts, only to find that we had now doubled our sandy beach--indeed we now had a "hill" of sand and it was downhill to the water instead of flat! Thank you, Lord! Now back to our story of our early ministry.

FILM GIVES WAY TO VIDEOS | We moved from East Vancouver to the quieter Tsawwassen, which gets less rain. As our ministry was established, we knew that the ministry should change gears, so to speak. We decided to put our energies to producing teaching videos so they could be shown at churches and sold to individuals, and cut down on our constant traveling. Over the years, we have produced, with the help of others, twelve teaching DVD's, which are shown in churches internationally. Most of them now minister on U tube and have become an internet outreach. The work goes on.

WHEELS | We did always have a small RV to travel in as I needed to cook our own food and have our own sleeping arrangements, especially as I was often sick and in pain at night. I used so much energy speaking and praying at meetings that I had no strength left for visiting after, as people expected if we stayed in their home. I often said to myself that if I didn't control my pain, then my pain would control me. God always gave me strength to minister, even when I felt unwell. I am a person who enjoys solitude, but rarely had any with the family and the ministry. I treasured the time I could be alone for prayer and bible research, and script writing. I rejoice now that I finally have more solitude time.

We missed the slower pace of life we enjoyed in Nelson. My parents were getting older at the time, and we longed to return to our beloved Kootenays. We were blessed to benefit from the rising prices in real estate at the Coast. We continued our international ministry, and still ministered on radio and television, and limited most of our traveling to conferences. We moved into a large, comfortable home in Nelson. Our two remaining children graduated high school in Nelson and within another couple of years they had moved to the West Coast. Alone at last! We converted our Nelson home into a triplex to generate income.

My original house in Balfour beckoned to us, some twenty miles into the countryside. We built on an addition and added a large dormer to the A frame upstairs. Our ministry moved into a building, once a fruit shed, and Keith built a garage onto it. We enjoyed our time in the country, close to my Mom and Dad. We travelled in our RV many times to be involved in our various outreaches by film, especially in California and Arizona. We attended conferences and spoke in California, Oregon, Pennsylvania, Missouri, Washington, Florida, and other States and Provinces.

PUBLICATION | While in Balfour, I wrote my first book, "Coping With the Cults" on an early Atari computer, and Harvest House published it, along with my next book, "What You Need to Know About Jehovah's Witnesses". All proceeds went into the ministry, even my royalties. Our outreach via our quarterly Magazine also filled up our days with research, handling orders, running our printshop, and answering mail. We also engaged in unique outreaches.

Chapter Sixteen

THE UNITED KINGDOM | When "Coping with the Cults" was published we went on a ministry trip to the United Kingdom, Scotland, and Wales. I had requested a small RV and one was provided. It was severely underpowered, with a four-cylinder motor. Our first overnight stop was to be in a "caravan park" in Sherwood Forest.

We were very jet lagged and longed to rest, but the resident "caretaker" marched us all over the park, barking orders. One building was for washing hair only. Another location was for dumping sani-toilets only, another for showers, another for toilets. We finally got our nap. I remarked that she reminded me of a jailhouse warden. Imagine how we chuckled when we walked by her residence later and saw a prominent sign "The Warden". Turns out the roof leaked on our RV overhead bed. We spent two months cuddled up on the table bed, narrow, but dry.

The dampness was constant in that rainy climate and we were grateful for a small catalytic heater. We got used to the lineups each morning. One to get milk or dairy products, another to buy bread, and yet another for food. Finally, one for the daily newspaper. We were thankful that in some locations stores similar to our grocery stores were just opening, and we could do one-stop shopping. I loved the English "clotted cream" and fresh produce stands.

We had some strange meals. At one home a buffet was set out which consisted of crisps (potato chips), fish sticks, and licorice allsorts. We filled our plates and sat huddled around the gas heater in the "lounge" (living room). Thank God for our RV (caravan) and a warm place to spend the nights.

Whoever set up our itinerary had us crisscrossing the country, only to double back, so we saw a lot of the UK! One early morning we pulled into the Mormon temple in Southern England and got there so early the Temple

Workers were seen by us in their all-white garments. They were mortified and quickly ran away. "Gentile" eyes are never to see the garments. We were able to share Christ with one of the men working at the Visitors Center. He had been a Baptist and had tears in his eyes as we left. May the Holy Spirit call him back to the faith he once had.

LONDON | While spending two months in the UK on our "maze" tour, we had arranged to touch base with our friends from Jeremiah Films who had an apartment in London. I wanted to go about thirty extra miles via a "ring road" to reach their apartment, but Keith insisted on the shortest route, through the heart of London. The traffic was unreal, especially with us driving on the "wrong" side of the road in our underpowered RV, with London taxis cutting in and out around us, while we tried to navigate. Impossible!

We were swept along against our will, over a bridge, and finally found a place to pull off, near a petrol station. "Lost" does not begin to describe our dilemma. We had gone miles on roads with names we could not find on our map. Keith took our map and joined the lineup at the Petrol Station. A man in the lineup asked if he could help us. Keith showed him our planned destination. We were within two blocks and easily completed the trip. We are sure an angel must have helped us! It was a wild ride we'll never forget!

LAND OF THE SCOTS | Entering Scotland we had a very special experience. Keith and I both have ancestral roots in Scotland and felt great anticipation entering that country. We passed the stone marker which said "Scotland" and pulled off into a large parking area. There stood a lone piper playing the bagpipes. We stood transfixed as he played and both agreed we felt our blood stir. What an outstanding welcome for those with Scottish blood.

Some minutes later a large tour bus pulled into the parking area and the piper rushed over to serenade them. Never mind, we had our special welcome for which we are grateful to the Lord. We were able to fit in the usual tourist sites between our speaking engagements and even visited a museum with one of Keith's father's paintings on display. We also researched our families at the clan centre, Keith's being royal with ties to Rob Roy MacGregor. Mine turned out to be border raiders and rather disreputable. Nevertheless, we both had our clan crests custom made, and we treasure them to this day.

My health, as usual, was not the best on this trip. I did end up in emergency one time. I was recovering in the RV and looked out the window in Glasgow. I remember saying to Keith, "the sky is grey, the buildings are grey, even the people are grey. I want to go home! When we did finish the tour we flew into Toronto and I was so encouraged to see all the houses of different colors as we flew in, and travelled across the country back to BC.

EPIPHANY: SALVATION THROUGH THE TABLOIDS | Back home, during one of my difficult nights when I couldn't sleep, I used the time to pray about how to reach more Jehovah's Witnesses for Christ. The idea popped into my head to advertise in the personal want ads of the Farmer's Almanac and various "scandal sheets" in the supermarkets, as well as "blanket" ads in various newspapers. I included the local papers in the vicinity of Watchtower headquarters in New York. What a harvest these small ads reaped over the years!

"Jehovah's Witnesses, families, and friends, find out facts the Society won't tell you. Free, Confidential" (followed by our Post Office box numbers in Canada and the USA).

Thousands of JW's and their families were reached with the gospel. We hope to meet some of these people in heaven one day!

DIGITAL | Along with our ministry partners we also set up one of the earliest websites to educate folks about Jehovah's Witnesses, Mormons, and other groups. As the technical, electronic age came about, we discontinued our ads and the snail mail they generated, making much more information available on our website, free to download.

We also subdivided my original homestead property at Balfour to provide income in the future from lot sales. God has always provided financing for us to be volunteers in the ministry by our "flipping" of houses, giving us mostly tax-free proceeds to meet our expenses and leaving the ministry money for outreach. We always tithed to our local church, as we knew "you can't out give God". We did not directly appeal for ministry funds, but God laid it on people's hearts to help us, including an American foundation that gifted charities with grants. We were the one and only Canadian outreach to receive these very welcome funds. Our ministry needs were always met. We were careful stewards of the money God placed in our hands.

HONOR YOUR MOTHER AND FATHER | It was time for my parents to relocate to a less demanding property. They sold their house and we moved them into a comfortable three-bedroom house on the main floor at one of our rental properties in Nelson. It soon became apparent that we needed to be closer to them, so we sold our Balfour house and one lot on which it sat, and found a fixer-upper two blocks from Mom and Dad. We finished the basement into a ministry facility, added a deck, new kitchen and bathroom, and moved the staircase to have an open-concept living room and dining room. When completed, it was a beauty, and we lived comfortably there for eleven years, busy in the ministry every day, until we turned the ministry over to our partners and retired to Langley (so we thought!). When Mom and Dad needed more care, we built on an addition to our home to accommodate them, which they enjoyed for ten years.

Chapter Seventeen

ON THE ROAD | Now I want to share some outstanding experiences we had during our years of ministry, that stand out in our minds and show the goodness of God in our lives. We travelled extensively in Canada and the USA, Australia, New Zealand, and the UK over thirty years. Here are some of our adventures, at home and abroad.

THE ROLLOVER | In all our years of travel, we had only two instances of RV trouble. We were driving in Oregon over an area that was rolling small hills. Keith had gone to the back of the RV Van conversion and stretched out on the bed, while I continued driving. I noticed that early Spring weather had caused slush on the tops of the hills and the last one seemed to have ice under the slush. I yelled back to Keith, "should I turn the cruise control off?" He didn't answer, but got up, sat in the passenger seat and clicked the seat belt on before he had even sat down properly. One of his legs was still between our two seats.

Upon the "click" we were into a full spin on the ice. The cruise control was still on as I went automatically into "skid mode", which meant you didn't touch the brakes but tried to steer out of the skid. We slid onto the gravel shoulder and the Van began to roll over down a grassy slope. An angel must have directed that roll over as we came to a rest back on our wheels, landing between two power poles, missing them both.

We looked behind us and saw a gory murder scene with ketchup splashed all over the interior. The full length mirror mounted on our closet door had broken into many strips that looked like lightening bolts and had imbedded themselves in our bed. Keith could have been easily impaled, had he not moved when he did. The only "injury" was to my thigh where his free-swinging leg had kicked me, and left a sizable bruise.

We had cried out "Jesus!" over and over as we rolled, and we thanked our Lord with a fervent prayer when we came to a stop. A passing vehicle called the police and a tow truck soon had us out of the ditch. We called our insurance company who authorized us to do a minimum "patch up" so we could continue on with our planned trip. We had to have the wheels realigned, a patch put over an overhead window, and a small propane part put on our motor. Off we went, shaken but grateful to God.

HELICOPTER CRASH | In Oregon, South of Bend, we were traveling North through patchy fog. I thought I spotted a small store where we could get some milk. Keith pulled over very briefly as I ascertained that the store was closed. We continued on a short distance and could hear some strange noises coming from above the RV. All of a sudden a small commuter helicopter dropped out of the sky onto the highway a short distance in front of us. We believe it would have landed on top of us if we had not had that brief delay.

Another truck was near us and we both stopped to rescue the pilot and passenger. The woman in the truck was a nurse and we dragged the injured passenger carefully to the side of the road, and she took care of him. Oncoming traffic was a real hazard due to the fog so we had to bring the occupants to safety and drag the helicopter wreckage to a safer place, a wide turning lane into a closed facility. Then Keith and the truck driver went to direct traffic around the accident scene, one on each end. That left me with a traumatized young pilot who proved very difficult to control. He was bleeding profusely from a head wound and it was all I could do to bring him into our RV so I could administer first aid.

It took a whole roll of paper towels to sop up the blood and then I had no bandages large enough to close his wound. I had to improvise with strips of tea towels and duct tape, but got the bleeding stopped. He was shaking and I wrapped our best real wool blanket around him, and tried to calm him down. He kept jumping up, pushing me aside and running out to the helicopter wreckage, mindless of traffic. Finally the police and ambulance arrived and were amazed at how four strangers had handled the dangerous situation. My last struggle with the young man was to get him to return our blanket (a family heirloom) in exchange for one the ambulance had for him. Thanks be to God for His presence with us through this traumatic time.

STRANDED | Just recently we had a tire blow out in a remote area of the Tiger Pass in Washington. There was a loud, earth shaking noise and we pulled off the road in one of the very few pull-off areas and got out. There was a loud hissing noise and a strong propane smell.

We quickly cut the motor and turned off the propane tank. We had foolishly been driving with the propane on for our fridge as I had stocked up on groceries.

There was no cell phone signal. We had just passed the last of the houses and ahead was seven miles of uninhabited road. Again, our prayers went out to the Lord to help us on this low traffic road. A strange-looking man, best described as "scraggly" came walking along the road towards us. As he got closer we saw that he was heavily tattooed and had many facial piercings. Wild hair and a beard completed the picture. His clothes hung on a skinny frame. Not exactly what one hopes to see in times of trouble!

However, he was carrying a landline phone receiver. We introduced ourselves and he pointed out a decrepit trailer in the nearby bush at the end of a long, winding access trail. He said there was a "hot spot" on the trail where we could phone for assistance. Keith insisted I go with him. After giving Keith a profoundly dirty look, I departed. Sure enough, he was as good as his word and I called a tire company to come out and change the tire for us.

We had a long wait and our new friend waited with us. He asked me if I knew anything about spiritual experiences which he was having and were troubling him. I was able to share with him about his occult experiences and direct him to the gospel message. He said he wanted to think about it, but he thought he would give Jesus a try.

At this moment the tow truck arrived and pointed out to us the dire danger we had been in. The blown tire had long metal pieces flying out from it, and one had cut the propane line when it blew. He pointed out the slightest spark could have blown us to "kingdom come". Usually the metal strips hanging from the tire cause a spark off the pavement which causes an explosion. Now we remembered the burnt out RV skeletons we had sometimes passed on the side of the road, and were extra thankful to God for our not being one of them. We now keep our propane fridge turned off when traveling!

Chapter Eighteen

REJOICING IN THE HARVEST | Looking back, one of our happiest times occurred when we met a young couple who were about to be baptized into the Jehovah's Witnesses. They were fervent and prepared to enter the full time "pioneer" ministry. They longed to serve God with all their hearts. A Christian lady had purchased our video, "The Witness at your Door" and showed it to them. They were blown away to find out we lived just a few miles from them and I invited them over. This was the first step in their conversion to Christ and we nurtured them along in their Christian growth over time. Their desire to serve God full time was realized when they became Pastors, eventually planting an evangelical church in the midst of the large Doukabor population in the Slocan Valley. Their outreach is prospering, and we feel like proud parents! To God be the glory!

IN THE HOME | While in our various locations in Canada, we offered a unique service to Christians. When the JW's or Mormons called, we told them to set up a future visit and we would happen to drop in, and they would receive a first-hand lesson in how to talk to these dear folks deceived by cult doctrine. In the Vancouver area, since I was on TV weekly, and our teaching videos were in circulation, I was often recognized and the JW's would jump up and run because I was considered an "evil slave" for leaving the organization. Keith carried on by himself and had many interesting encounters, both with me and by himself.

MILITANT ELDERS | One day, my Mom and Dad were visiting our home when the JW's blundered in (their territory card usually blacklisted our house as "do not call"). My Dad invited them back to talk to "his daughter". When they arrived, I was in disguise, with a head full of pink curlers, no makeup, and my gardening clothes. The JW elder asked me if I was "Bill Robison's daughter?" I said "yes. Please come in." We shared with them at length and were clearly winning the biblical "discussion" when one of them became suspicious and pressed me as to whether I had ever been a JW.

Keith and I had become very skilled at dodging this question. Even if the JW's asked me, Keith would loudly proclaim, "I was never a Jehovah's Witness" I came out of the Baptist Church. I would remain silent and usually the moment passed. However, if the JW's persisted in asking me, I would launch into our family history, about how my Grandfather and our family were early JW's (International Bible Students/ Millennial Dawn) and how the Organization had missed the end of the world in 1925. Often they got caught up and forgot that I hadn't actually answered the question about myself.

However, these two were not to be stopped by our usual tactics and I had to answer their direct question. They were rising and hurling insults at me as they prepared to leave. Keith snuck out to their fancy car, around to the front bumper and stuck a bumper sticker on that said "Jehovah's Witnesses are False Prophets". They got in their car and drove off. We found out later that they were puzzled on the way home by some people pointing at them as they drove through town. They drove into their garage and still didn't spot the sticker. We heard it made quite a commotion when they drove into the Kingdom Hall Parking Lot the next morning and the whole congregation spotted it!

They later called at a local Pastor's home and he had a profound discussion with them, being well prepared by the classes we had taught at his church. We provided a good supply of our literature. One plants, another waters, and God makes it grow! (1 Corinthians 3:7)

OBNOXIOUS ENCOUNTER | A Christian lady had encountered a JW neighbor, and we were called in for a visit. The JW lady was truly one of the most obnoxious we had ever encountered, constantly and rudely interrupting every time we tried to speak. Finally, just before we left, I turned to her and said, "Your organization is so disrespectful of Jesus Christ, not only have they altered their Bible everywhere Scripture teaches Jesus Christ is God, but they refer to the Christ child as "it" not "he". That briefly caught her attention just as we were leaving. In the car, we prayed for her as we do for everyone we talk to, but at the end of our prayer I foolishly asked the Lord for His forgiveness for wasting our time and His!

Our post-encounter prayer is what we affectionately call "the Holy Ghost Miserables Prayer". We know we are mere witnesses of the gospel message, so we always pray first before the encounter, that the cult deception will be bound in Jesus' name so the person can hear the Word of God. It is the Holy Spirit that convicts people, not us. We also pray after we leave that the Holy Spirit will make them so miserable with their false cult doctrine that they will turn to the real Jesus Christ. This prayer works!

Two years later the Christian lady that had introduced us to this militant JW told us an amazing story. Apparently this JW was extremely bothered that the Christ child was called "it" in the JW bible. She reported that she thought about it most days and especially at night in bed, and this finally led to her being so miserable she decided to find out once and for all if the JW bible was indeed corrupt as we had claimed. The Christian lady had lots of our literature and helped this JW come to Christ and then to Church. They were now fast friends! Praise God! Thank you, Holy Spirit!

CONFRONTATION | On another one of these home encounters there was an older JW who claimed to be of the elite 144,000 heavenly class. His arrogant attitude was evident as he ridiculed the Deity of Christ, the Trinity, participation in the military, and especially the Christian belief in Hell. We countered him with Scriptures, asking, "If this is what you believe as a JW, could you please explain this scripture?" We have seen Hebrews 4:12 in action many times before, *"For the word of God is living and active and sharper than any two-edged sword, and piercing as far as the division of soul and spirit, of both joints and marrow, and able to judge the thoughts and intentions of the heart"*.

He tried time and again to turn to his Watchtower publications and read to us, but we pointed out that we were using only the Bible to talk to him, and surely he, as "God's anointed" could use only the Bible to reply to us. He couldn't. Finally he jumped up, greatly agitated, and pounded on his Watchtower Bible, exclaiming, "If the Watchtower Society is wrong, and there is a hell, then I will go to hell with the Watchtower Society"! I replied, "Have a nice trip. Jesus doesn't send anyone to hell, they choose to go".

We prayed for him after he left that the Holy Spirit would bring to his mind the Scriptures we had shared with him. The next time the householder had a visit from him, she reported that he was extremely twitchy and kept asking, "are they coming?" She reported that his whole countenance changed from arrogant and superior to nervous. We are sure our prayers, (leaving him in the charge of the Holy Spirit) will produce results, in God's time.

LDS | One day a couple of Mormon missionaries showed up at our door, when we were living in the country. We shared with them for a couple of hours, and then invited them to stay for supper. We had meatloaf as a main course and apple pie for dessert. I looked up to see one of the young men with tears running down his face and dripping off his chin. I immediately went to him and hugged him as he sobbed out how lonely he was for his family back in Utah and I cooked just like his Mother. The dominant Mormon looked disgusted.

After supper the other young Mormon, who was on the arrogant side the whole time, challenged us by saying, "If you believe so strongly that the Mormons are deceived, why aren't you on TV telling the whole world?" "Just a minute, Keith replied, you are right and there is something I want you to see."

He adjusted our satellite dish and the John Ankerberg Show was just coming out of Tennessee with me as his guest, promoting my book, "Coping with the Cults" and discussing the chapter on Mormonism. They just stood there in open-mouthed amazement but fled when I stated their Prophet Joseph Smith was a false prophet. I have since learned, that if we want to keep the Mormons around to hear the gospel, don't criticize Joseph Smith! There are plenty of other gospel topics to share.

IT'S THE MORMONS! | We sent our restless children off to see the matinee performance of "Battlestar Galactica". Randy remarked on returning that, "Mom, it's just the Mormons! That movie is just the Mormons". We poo-poohed this idea, but found out later that he was right! This movie did have a distinct Mormon connection.

Randy is now a successful businessman in his forties but still witnesses regularly to the cults and shares his Christian faith. He sits next to us in church, along with his glowing Christian teenage daughter. We are so blessed to live in the in law suite in his home and know we will be given loving care in our old age, just as we cared for my parents.

RELATIONSHIPS | One of his employees was a Jehovah's Witness of long standing, but is also a close friend who visits regularly, with his JW wife. Upon meeting Keith and I, we also became friends. He had recently lost his Mother and asked if I would be his "Mom" as Randy was like his brother. I am very fond of this couple, and of course agreed. We have many discussions and I back up everything I say with the original publications of the Watchower Society. He has never asked me directly if I was a JW, and I have never told him (other than the story of my family and 1925). They even travelled 400 miles to visit us at our Lake lot.

Finally the elders at the Kingdom Hall wised up that they were losing him and so forbid this couple to associate with Randy and us. He tried, but he was so drawn to the love of Christ that fills our home that they kept coming back. They ended up being disfellowshipped out of the WT Society. After so many years and his family's involvement, this has been a hard time for them. We know they have the "Holy Ghost Miserables" and even admit to this, but we are still waiting on the Lord to see how long it takes before they turn to Jesus fully. We are but witnesses, the Spirit draws. We wait.

LEAVE ME ALONE! | In desperation at a "Mormon Onslaught" a lady called us to come as the Mormons kept returning and she wanted to end the visits. Most Mormon missionaries are polite, but one of these three seemed to be very pushy and had "angry eyes". We wondered why there were three, but we were soon to find out! As I opened my Bible to read some portion of scripture which corrected their presentation, I looked up to see a violent man coming at me in attack mode, stepping on the coffee table and grabbing my bible. I held on for dear life, and the other two Mormons grabbed my attacker and wrestled him out to the hallway and left the building. It was scary, but the lady got her wish. They did not return.

CLOSET MORMONS | During one of our many residential moves, I was cleaning out closets before moving in. We found out the previous owner was the head Mormon in the area, so said some extra prayers over our house before moving in. At the back of a closet I found several pages of names and addresses. All the mormons in the area, in fact. We wasted no time in sending out gospel tracts exposing Mormonism to every name on the list. Thank you Lord!

DIGITAL MORMONS | That was not the only Mormon list God provided for us. A Christian janitor in one of the large States found a discarded list of all the Mormons in that State and sent it on to us. We mailed out hundreds of gospel tracts exposing Mormonism and presenting the real Jesus Christ and His message of salvation by grace. It is in God's hands.

CONVENTION OUTREACH | A wealthy businessman with a heart for the cults, took his Secretary to one of the large conventions held each year by Jehovah's Witnesses. They wrote down the car license plate for every car in the parking lot, and then he did a search for each one. I believe the searches were about $3.50 each at the time. We received a major pile of computer printouts which provided us with names and addresses. We called in our volunteers, divided up the piles of names, stuffed envelopes and wrote addresses in our own handwriting. (People are more likely to open them). We filled up Canada Post's largest mail sack with these letters and mailed them all at once. Our ministry friend paid the considerable postage as well. Our fervent prayers followed these outreaches with the gospel.

CHRISTIAN TELEVISION | Over the years, some seven times, we were invited on the 100 Huntley Street Christian TV program, viewed coast-to-coast in Canada and some of the States. This always generated much mail, but our first appearance was special. I received a response from a young mother who had been influenced by Jehovah's Witnesses. She had prayed the Sinner's prayer and received Christ through one of her friends, but still needed nurturing to get rid of the Watchtower influence. We began our snail mail correspondence (before the days of computers!). All my previous JW friends had forsaken me due to the cruel shunning practices of the Watchtower Society, and I longed for a true friend.

LINDA | Over time, we talked on the phone and finally met. She became, in her own words, "a heavy duty Christian". Not only a talented musician, composer and singer, she also began to do presentations on the cults in churches and was a reliable resource for local ministry as we needed her. We visited over the years in each others homes and went through many trials of faith together.

Her beautiful daughter was killed in a car accident. Linda went to the family of the responsible young man and offered them forgiveness and God's salvation message. They are in God's Kingdom today. How often we clung together in earnest prayer, our hearts breaking for each other. How often we rejoiced together over souls saved, and needs met. I rejoice in Linda's happiness in her late-in-life marriage to a mature, Christian man. I know first hand how special it is to have a husband who is also a ministry partner.

Linda is a "forever friend", just like my faithful friend Trudy. Our relationship spans decades and is still going strong! Trudy was my neighbor and our friendship grew despite her being an unbeliever and I a JW. In time, with both of us born again, Trudy served faithfully with us in the ministry. I also mention longtime friends, Wendy, Muriel, and Joan and several new acquaintances, all of whom are a blessing to me, and a gift from God. Our Balfour neighbors, Elly and Gerda, are special friends as well.

Chapter Nineteen

TARGETED SCIENTOLOGY | Following the release of my first book, "Coping With the Cults", which went into six printings, the cults named in that book weren't too happy with me. Scientology got only a brief mention exposing their doctrine and their leader as false. At that time Scientology was suing everyone who dared to criticize them in any way. I was "saved" by being a Canadian. They could not sue me without going through our Canadian RCM Police. One came for a brief investigation and I showed the Police I was quoting correct sources. I was being factual, not hateful, nor committing slander. The Police suggested I remove the small section on Scientology from my book index and I agreed to do so with the next printing. We had just received a new shipment of 1,000 books, so I knew the Scientology movement would not receive any instant gratification, That ended the matter.

THE WORLDWIDE CHURCH OF GOD | The Worldwide Church of God was another matter. Herbert W. Armstrong, their Founder and Prophet was still alive. I exposed his false doctrine of God being a "family" and all believers who were faithful, eventually joining that "family" in heaven. The Trinity and the Deity of Christ were denied by this group at that time. When we were traveling in the UK I noticed a prominent display of their "Plain Truth" magazine in the airport. It featured a sign, saying "Free, Help Yourself". I couldn't resist helping myself to the contents of the magazine rack and consigning them to the garbage disposal. I shared this experience in our "MacGregor Ministries News & Views" magazine. I even suggested that since we were told to "help ourselves", that readers could follow my example and keep the magazines out of the hands of the unsuspecting public.

Sure enough, here came the RCMP again, bringing our magazine as "evidence" against me. Their whole case collapsed when I admitted to taking their magazines, at their invitation, but never in Canada, only Overseas. The RCMP considered laying a charge of "mischief" against me (a $200 fine) at that time, but I had committed no offense in Canada, so they couldn't bring charges. I told them I would not pay any fine and if they were going to continue then they would have to arrest me. My one phone call would be to our contacts in the media who would document the whole matter far and wide.

The young officer became very uncomfortable and contacted his superiors for advice. I was told I would have to print a "retraction" of my advice, since disposing of a whole rack of magazines was an offense in Canada. The WCG apparently paid merchants to place their racks. I was single-handedly responsible for the WCG changing their signs to allow one free copy per rack.

My "retraction" advised readers to avail themselves of their one free copy of the "Plain Truth" magazine and dispose of them, one by one. The matter was dropped.

Imagine my surprise some time later to hear from the headquarters of the WCG, after Herbert W. Armstrong's death, asking me to review their doctrine on God. The new leadership were determined to make sure all their doctrines were biblical. I entered into a process of being one of the helpers who assisted the WCG into a correct, biblical understanding of the nature of God. They had also contacted several Bible Colleges and scholars to help them. Together, with the help of the Holy Spirit, we had the privilege of seeing a cult turn into a Christian denomination. Truly unique!

We were invited to their Headquarters and spent most of a day with them, touring the very elaborate premises, discussing spiritual topics, and encouraging them on the path they had taken, the pursuit of truth. The leadership tried their best with their followers, but becoming "born again" is an individual transaction between the one person and Jesus Christ. They were trying to corporately get their members "born again" as a group. They were therefore facing problems with those who wanted the "old ways", and withheld their tithes. It would be necessary for them to sell the very valuable real estate on which their opulent headquarters sat, and relocate to less expensive headquarters, which they eventually did. The buildings, sculptures, paintings, fountains, and elegant theatre (celebrating the ego of the founding prophet, Herbert W. Armstrong,) were sold. Many split-off groups loyal to the original prophet formed and continue their cult heritage, but the Worldwide Church of God continues on, much smaller and much more biblical.

Chapter Twenty

AUSTRALIA | Keith and I were excited to be going on our first-ever overseas ministry tour to Australia, mainly sponsored by the Assemblies of God in Australia via a Canadian Pastor who endorsed us. After a long, uncomfortable flight overnight to Australia, we found we were booked for that evening! Never mind the eighteen-hour time difference apparently! We were told they had a special treat for us, being from Canada.

Our car journey took us around and around a mountain, climbing all the while. I was already feeling slightly motion sick from the extended flying, and prayed I would hold down my food. The driver pulled triumphantly up to the scraggliest maple tree we had ever seen and proudly showed us the few red and yellow leaves, (a rare sight indeed in Australia) a Canadian maple tree. We didn't have the heart to tell him that we lived in an area of tall, magnificent, giant maple trees whose fall foliage was breath-taking, the best the world had to offer!

Despite our exhaustion and jet lag, God was faithful to get us through the unexpected meeting and safely back down the mountain to the home where we were staying. We were served the usual night time snack of tea and toast with Vegemite. An acquired taste for sure, since it is apparently a byproduct of yeast. I got used to it, but Keith never did. We fell into bed exhausted, to the whirl of fans in the tropical heat. We finally fell asleep in our strange surroundings only to be jarred awake at 4 a.m. by the maniacal laughter of the Cuckaborro bird. A rude awakening indeed to begin our tour!

While we enjoyed the many beautiful birds in Australia, every color of the rainbow, we were always jarred by their loud and piercing voices. The exception was the bell bird who make a sound just like the ringing of a clear bell. This occurs in only one small location in all of Australia, only occasionally, and we were warned that we may have made the hike for nothing, as many leave disappointed. However, God was gracious and we didn't have long to wait to hear the amazing voice of the bell bird. We were relieved to return to Canada and be awakened by the sweet, musical tweeting of our much smaller but not so glamorous bird population.

VISION | While waiting at the airport for our return flight to Canada, we went to a snack area and sat down at a small table. As I raised my eyes to the wall, I was shocked to see the "vision" I had just before being assigned the main sanctuary in Nelson for our Bible class, a few years previously. That vision had been a dark blue background with some stars I now recognized the Southern Constellation called the Southern Cross. The five stars, representing the five Australian states. An angel had taken me from star to star in my vision, and I had wondered what it all meant. Now I knew! We ministered in all five Australian States eventually. Visions like this have not happened since, but it makes me feel blessed to recall the experience and see the hand of the Lord in our lives. More was to come.

Over our three visits in all, we enjoyed time spent with Koala bears, platypuses, and pie-snatching Emus, taller than us. As we travelled we saw many kangaroos and abandoned camels in the wild. We drove over many roads and looked way up to markers showing the high water mark from the previous years' floods. The water tasted bad for the most part, so we developed the Aussie habit of drinking large quantities of delicious juices in the heat. I believe I gave myself high blood sugar at this time I could hardly eat, as I had little appetite for lamb, the main meal in that country.

DIET | On our first tour, we were served lamb every day, prepared the same way. The lamb would be roasted with potatoes and pumpkin chunks soaking up the grease beside it. I struggled every day to choke down a few bites, as the distinctive flavor of the lamb tasted the same to me as the wild venison I had to endure in my unhappy days in the past. I had made a vow to never again eat wild meat,and had kept it, until Australia and its venison/lamb/mutton flavor tested my resolve.

The only other flavor I hated was curry, which I was forced to eat as a child. We finally ended up at a home where the woman said to me "I bet you're tired of eating roasted lamb every day, aren't you? I have a special treat for you". My words of gratitude died on my lips as she triumphantly brought in curried lamb.

Before our next tour I sent out word that we did not eat lamb, and we were so thankful for the alternative meals we were served. We now have a good laugh over this scenario, but it took a while to stop twitching! Of course the Airline served lamb on the way home.

TRAVELING ALONG THE GOLD COAST | We stopped for lunch at an Australian burger stand. Keith placed his order, as usual, for a burger "with everything on it". When it arrived at our table, we were amazed to see a "tower" about a foot high. There was the thick burger all right, but it also had a fried egg, a ring of pineapple, a thick slice of cooked beet, as well as the usual onions, tomatoes, and lettuce. He had to divide it in two and compress the halves to get even half in his mouth!

CRITTERS | We also learned over the tours not to approach some interesting critters. There was a small green frog with red eyes that was so cute. I received a football tackle from the Pastor's wife to remove me from the deadly spit that could have ended my life. Snakes abounded in some areas, all of them poisonous, so we had to be diligent. A large beetle, the size of a mouse paid me a visit one day, but was harmless. Understandingly, it was called the hippopotamus (or was it rhinoceros) beetle. Huge cockroaches were everywhere and taught us to shake out our shoes every morning. Of course, a few bites from the dengue fever mosquito caused much suffering and its effects remain with me to this day. Any activity raising my body temperature caused the dengue symptoms to return. Hot flushes from menopause/dengue were especially uncomfortable.

THE GODMAKERS | We were anxious to have our first showing of the 16mm film exposing Mormonism, which we premiered throughout Australia and left behind for them. It was arranged for me to speak briefly on Sunday and then show our film on the Monday night. The Head Pastor was on holidays in Hawaii, but there were several other Pastors on staff for the large church of 2,500. A new addition was built, almost ready for full use on the side of the already large church.

We arrived at the church about an hour early on Monday night. To our surprise, the parking lot was full and we were met at the gate by a frazzled worker who tried to turn us away, explaining they would ask the speakers from Canada to have a second showing, if they were willing. We explained we were those speakers, so were let in. Talk about a full house and just as many waiting outside! The film was shown to the "standing room only" crowd. The audience was asked to move into the addition and I would do the question and answer period following. The addition was quickly full, a mike was rigged up and we held our lively session while the second group saw the movie, again filling the church to capacity.

We then returned to the original auditorium to begin the question and answer period for them. We had many good questions as attendants ran about with live mikes. All was going well when a lady stood up and asked, "If the Mormons wear their special temple underwear next to their bodies, and then their underclothes on top, how do they have sex?" I heard several gasps of disbelief from the line of Pastors behind me. I replied "appropriate slits, next question please". Sighs of relief could be heard from the Pastors.

We found out later that the Pastor phoned from Hawaii to see how the showing had gone. He exclaimed, "They filled my church two times on a MONDAY night! What is she doing now? The Pastor replied that I was holding up a pair of Mormon Temple Underwear. I don't know if he cut his trip short, but he was back within a couple of days.

The meeting finally ended and the crowd moved out to our book table, which Keith was manning as best he could. I remained behind at the stage as I usually do for those wanting prayer.

Finally only one man remained and he was scary. He was very large and covered with tattoos. We were alone. He approached me with a scowl on his face and demanded that I hand over the sacred temple underwear which I had no business having. I ran from him up onto the stage, put the temple underwear under me, and sat down on it, taking a firm grip on the arms of the chair, and prayed "Jesus, help me!" I wasn't going to give up that underwear without a struggle. I fixed my steeliest stare on him, trying to show no sign of fear, as he loomed over me. He hesitated just long enough for a couple of deacons to come back into the sanctuary wondering why I was taking so long, I called out to them to come up to the front. The man glared at me and hastily left. God is good. The underwear travelled with us all over Australia, North America, and the United Kingdom, and we have recently donated them to an active Mormon ministry.

THE BOOK STORE | The boxes of books, cassette tapes, and literature we had shipped on ahead that were supposed to last for the entire tour, sold out at the first meeting in Brisbane. The demand was so great for our literature at the Australian meetings that the AOG church in Brisbane put their print shop at our disposal and helped us out. We established an office in Australia before we left. Everyone seemed to know us when we arrived, and we found out that someone had taken my testimony tape into the country and it had been duplicated far and wide. We promised to return, and did, two more times.

MINISTERING ANGEL | I still get goosebumps when I think of one adventure on the other side of the world, far from family and friends. We were driving our rental car in Australia down the Gold Coast to a very busy schedule in Sydney, Australia. We had a stopover on the way. Keith bent down to tie his shoe and his back seized up and he could not move without much pain. Our schedule was so tight we could not linger to seek medical help. We managed to get him into the car. I was terrified to drive on the "wrong" side of the road and he felt he could still drive, as long as he didn't move too much.

We carried on to Sydney to the Pastor's home where we were to stay for one night. Keith went immediately to bed and barely moved for the next week. We prayed constantly for his muscle spasms to let up. He knew from previous experience that he had to just wait this situation out. We got some pain pills, but they didn't help much. We cried out to the Lord for help because Keith drove me to all the meetings, and also looked after the book table and helped with prayers and ministry after. We were a team and I could not handle the job alone. We cried out to the Lord to help us. The first meeting in Sydney was only hours away.

A knock came on the Pastor's door and there stood a young woman who had been a full-time pioneer for the Jehovah's Witnesses before coming to Christ. She said she had taken the week off work to go around to all the meetings we were having and could she be of any help to us? I cried with relief as I now had a chauffeur to all the meetings and she would look after the book table and help with ministry. Poor Keith was a victim of his bedridden misery and the Pastor and his wife graciously allowed us to stay with them till Keith could move. Our new friend was a Godsend and got me through the many meetings in diverse locations. Our time in Sydney was finally drawing to an end.

NIGHTMARE | The next leg of our journey was supposed to be a car trip to the next State, and then we would fly out of there to continue on. We saw the same car rental logo at our destination so assumed we could drive there and turn our rental car in there. It came as a big shock to find out that we could not cross State lines with the rental car, but that it must be turned in at Sydney. We had to quickly find alternate travel arrangements that Keith could navigate.

Our efforts to get a bus ticket met with the same rules. There were no commuter airlines available for the relatively short trip. Only trains crossed State lines. Trouble was, there were no seats available for over three weeks. We put our names on the cancellation list, but there were about thirty people ahead of us. I phoned the train reservations every two hours, praying in between times that God would help us somehow. By the meeting time that night, I felt really defeated.

Here was my husband, barely able to move. Our helper had to go back to work. We had to leave the next day to keep our schedule. I went to the meeting with a heavy heart. The meeting went well but prayer time lasted a long time. I was exhausted and finally went to the book table to help our friend pack up. There were still quite a few people lingering around at the back. A man in a black suit walked up to me and said "this is for you", and handed me an envelope. I assumed he was one of the elders of that church giving me an honorarium. I put it in my purse.

I noticed my friend jumping up and trying to see into the last of the crowd. As we were packing up she said to me, "I don't know who that man was". This was her home church. She had tried to get a better look at him but couldn't seem to find him in the crowd. He "just disappeared" according to her. We shrugged and got packed up and back to our house.

Keith was in bed waiting for me to come home. He felt so helpless, and we really did not know what we were going to do. I sat on the bed and started sorting out the book table sales and the honorarium envelope so we could deposit into our bank through the post office the next day, as was our custom in travel around Australia. I tore open the envelope and saw two small tickets in the bottom. To our amazement they were two first class tickets on the train for the next morning to our planned destination!

We were so happy, and assumed that the Pastor of the church had been able somehow to get us these unavailable tickets. When we phoned him to thank him, he had no idea what we were talking about. He said he had tried everything to get us on the train, but had failed. He also had no idea who the man was who had given us the tickets! Our friend continued to inquire from everyone she knew at the various churches for some time into the future, and no one knew anything! All we knew was that God had heard our prayers and had intervened, so we were determined to be on that train. Some angels wear black suits!

The Pastor who had had us as unexpected guests for so long, continued to graciously help us. I gave him the rental car money and he arranged to return the car for us and take us to the train. Keith made a valiant effort, and by moving slowly along walls and other supports he got into the car and then into the train station, all in slow motion. The Pastor carried our heavy baggage and checked it through to our destination. He stayed to help Keith up the train steps and into our first class seats. We knew we were being met at the train station at our destination, so breathed a sigh of relief that we were on our way. The trip was comfortable in our first class roomy seats and we enjoyed the scenery on the way. It was a welcome and much needed rest.

Trouble was that the train stopped about a half hour before we reached our destination in the middle of a field some distance from a closed station, in the blazing noonday sun. We were told by loudspeaker that we would all have to disembark and walk to the waiting busses at the closed station, quite a distance from us. Everybody rushed off. Keith and I had to wait till they left the train, so we could get Keith out of his seat and down the difficult steps and finally onto the field. We were making our way in a slow shuffle across the field when, to our horror, we saw both busses leave in a cloud of dust.

We finally shuffled on to the abandoned platform, which thankfully still had its roof, so we could get out of the tropical sun. We knew someone had to notice at some point that we were not on the bus, and we would be rescued. We had no water and no food, and settled down on the platform floor to wait it out, praying for help. I remember thinking, "Really, Lord, what next?"

A REAL JOB'S COMPLAINT | I'll admit to a pity party as I waited. I reminded the Lord that He had divinely provided train tickets, so why had He now abandoned us in the hottest, loneliest place on earth, with no help on the horizon? It got hotter and hotter and more and more uncomfortable. I kept shading my eyes and looking up the dirt road. Finally I saw a small cloud in the sky. I felt like one of God's early prophets, Elijah who had prayed for rain and then seen a small cloud coming (1Kings 18:44). Could it be dust from a vehicle coming to rescue us? Sure enough, a very small red hatchback car drove up to the abandoned station, and a young man got out.

He had been sent by the church to pick us up at the train station, waited around for us, and then went to the baggage claim and was told we had not arrived to claim our baggage. He found out the details of what had happened and decided he had better drive out to the abandoned station and see if we had somehow failed to get on the bus.

We were overjoyed to be found, but he had loaded his small car with our baggage and there was very little room left for passengers. Keith could not bend himself to fit into the small car so we finally rearranged things, putting down the back seat and reclining the passenger seat as far back as it would go and finally stuffed Keith in somehow. The hatchback was filled with our baggage so we moved one suitcase onto Keith's lap, making a small space for me. By drawing up my knees and bending my head down, I managed to just fit in, and he shut the back hatch. We were so overloaded for that small car, I prayed the whole time we would make it! We were off in a cloud of dust and and arrived at our destination.

Again, obstacles presented themselves. The home we were assigned to stay in was at the top of a hill, accessible by a long, steep climb up many cement stairs. Those stairs made me feel like bursting into tears, as I knew what pain Keith would endure hauling himself up. Thank God for a sturdy handrail, and Keith's perseverance! We were finally at a place we could rest. We were also able to finally access some stronger muscle relaxant pills, a treatment for Keith, and he slowly became mobile over the next week.

Ultimately we made three trips to Australia of sixty days, ninety days, and one hundred and twenty days ministering from one end of the country to the other. This was before the days of cell phones, GPS's, digital discs, and other helpful items for the traveller. We premiered the 16 mm films, "The Godmakers" on the Mormons and "Witnesses of Jehovah" on the Jehovah's Witnesses in Australia, leaving those films behind to bless others in that country. These documentary films were causing quite a stir around the country.

ON NATIONAL TV | At one point we were in Adelaide, Australia speaking at the largest Assembly of God church in Australia, with over 4,000 in attendance. We were contacted by the news program "State Affair" shown nationally on the Australian Broadcasting Network, who wanted to do a segment on us. This was free publicity we could never have afforded and their reporter came out to interview us. They had such an unexpected response to our interview that they requested we come into their studio for a follow-up program. They asked if we could bring our films so they could input segments from the films into the interview. We agreed. We were isolated as soon as we got to the studio and were told we would be called when they were ready for us.

GLADIATORS | At the last moment before we went before the cameras they confessed that they had gathered all the cult members who had complained about us so they could confront us in person. They said they didn't tell us beforehand because they were sure we wouldn't have come. We assured them we were delighted with their format. We said a quick prayer for extra help from the Holy Spirit and went in to face our adversaries. The studio bleachers were full.

The only group not there were the Jehovah's Witnesses because they were not allowed to talk to an "evil slave" such as myself, who had willingly removed herself from 'Jehovah's Organization'. The Scientologists in attendance stood and said they would represent Jehovah's Witnesses as well as themselves. I had to stifle myself from smirking, as I could imagine how JW's would feel about Scientologists speaking for them! Many Mormons were there, including the local leaders and there was a good smattering of the other cults, especially the Christadelphians.

I was in my element, in the Lord's power and presence, and calmly and with authority responded to every attack, and even managed to ask questions they could not answer, and used their own quotes and many bible verses in my replies. God was truly with us. It was lively, informative, and a good time was had by us, but apparently not by them, judging by their storm-cloud faces!

Nevertheless, at the end of the encounter the host took an audience vote as to who had won the "debate". To our surprise, the majority voted that

Keith and I had won. The next day some cult members tracked us down and told us they had decided to leave that church after the encounter and handed over their tithe money! Because of the wide range of that program, everywhere we went people seemed to know of us, some labeling us the "cult busters from Canada". We saw so much fruit from our sharing in Australia, it seemed unimaginable. To God be the glory!

MAGNETIC ISLAND | On another trip, we flew into Northern Australia to minister there first and then go South to other parts of the country. We were surprised to be offered a free resort vacation on Magnetic Island for a few days. We were introduced to the local gourmet specialty "Morton Bay Bugs". Despite their name, they were delicious.

As we walked on the beach later, we noticed many warning signs. Very poisonous jelly fish were present on the sand and were virtually invisible, and should one step on them, they could die. Also, I received four very large mosquito bites on my arm that swelled up alarmingly and I became very ill. I spent the night on the floor of the bathroom watching the very large cockroaches scurry about, sure I was going to die right then, on the other side of the world, far from my family and friends. What next, God?!

I was shaky but able to carry on with our schedule, often having only the strength to get up and speak and then going to rest. I lost my appetite but drank lots of delicious juice. The water was not good, and there was no "bottled water" like today. No matter how sick I felt, when it was time for me to speak, I could feel God's power carrying me. I remember being so weak at times I had to have Keith carry my bible and put it on the podium for me. I believe that this is when my high blood sugar began, with all that juice drinking, and not much food eaten. I had gained weight over this time.

Having coped with constant pain and discomfort most of my life, I had steeled myself to act normally, no matter what I felt like. The years of practice with chronic pain helped me get through it all. I was very relieved to be finally heading home after ninety days on tour, having done 120 meetings, including several in New Zealand. We flew overnight to the Los Angeles airport, and were awaiting our flight to Vancouver, Canada.

ROUGH LANDING | I began to feel very ill at the airport. We walked outside trying to get some fresh air. The airport was under construction and I remember throwing up in a potted plant trying to make it to a restroom. I felt feverish and very unsteady. We slowly made it back to our boarding lounge and I headed for the ladies washroom. As I opened one stall door, I could no longer stand and fell to the floor. My purse landed behind me and I could not muster up enough strength to reach for it. People were stepping over me and my purse to use the other stalls. I couldn't believe the insensitivity of the people in Los Angeles. I was violently ill and remember having to lay my head on the dirty toilet seat, but I simply could not hold it up. I could not get up.

RECOVERY | Keith became concerned that I was taking so long and asked a lady to go in and check on me. She came back and reported that I was lying on the floor. Keith got the airline to call an ambulance, which they did. I was treated as a heart attack victim and was wheeled out onto the landing strip between two 747's, and put in the ambulance. Keith jumped in beside me. We taxied out on the runway with the 747's until we came to an emergency gate. It was surreal, looking up at the underbelly of a big jet with its engines running and hovering almost over us. We arrived in Emergency and I was immediately put on interveinous fluids. By the second large IV bottle I was starting to feel somewhat better.

The doctor told me he believed that I had a tropical disease of some kind and I needed to go home now that I was stabilized and go to a specialist in the field. I knew my troubles had started when we walked on the beach. We phoned a ministry friend and he came and rescued us and took us to Manhattan Beach where he lived and gave us some food and a place to sleep overnight. I was filthy from laying on the airport floor and violently throwing up. He came up with a pair of sweat pants he had found and an old tee shirt, so I was able to shower and wash out my travel clothes. Our suitcases had flown on without us to Vancouver. I put on my damp clothes the next day and we flew home to Vancouver, thankful that our suitcases were waiting. We still had to travel 400 miles to our home.

Once again, our ministry friends were a tremendous help so I could rest before the long drive home. They carried the ministry load at the West Coast, turning their basement into a mail order center and faithfully holding meetings for years. Upon retiring, they tried a move to Nelson, but ended up moving again to be closer to their family. We were once again on our own. We appreciate their faithfulness over the years.

As we lived in a small city without a specialist, again God intervened, as I struggled with dengue fever, just one of my health trials! A specialist in urology had moved to town and I was referred to him for bladder pain. He was lying on his floor when I went into his office. He said, "excuse me, but I have dengue fever and must wait for this episode to pass.' He immediately recognized my symptoms as dengue fever also, when I shared my experiences with him. So, God sent a tropical medicine doctor to me, when I could not find one in our Province. God is so faithful. I learned how to manage my tropical disease, since there is no cure.

Dengue fever is somewhat like malaria, but there is no drug that helps. When I did something to raise my body temperature, my type of dengue fever can reoccur and attack. I have controlled my attacks to this day by following his advice. I had the most unpleasant menopause imaginable as hot flashes triggered the dengue fever attacks, but praise God I lived through it. I refused to curtail ministry activities, daily quoting, "I can do all things through Christ, who strengthens me". (1 Tim. 1:12). He strengthened me, and few people knew what I was living through, thirty-five years of chronic pain and discomfort. Incidentally, I am now mostly pain free.

Chapter Twenty-One

THE GOVERNMENT TAKETH AWAY | Prior to 2008, the ministry had undergone a government audit after 30 years, and we were complimented on our absolutely "clean" books. However, Revenue Canada had changed their Charity laws. Charities had to comply or lose their Charity status. We were aware of these changes, but felt that our national charity, MacGregor Ministries, was "grandfathered in", since it had functioned since 1981 and met every requirement.

A couple from Edmonton, who had run a support group for ex-JW's decided to retire to Nelson and help us. We joined our two ministries and they purchased a Nelson home in preparation for a move. The house was bought at a bargain price, then real estate values escalated rapidly. Keith and I looked after the rental for them. When things began to go badly with our charity status we offered to release them from their promises, help them to sell the house, and they would realize a tidy profit.

They declined our offer and decided to retire to Nelson anyway. A very pro-JW Government auditor was determined to shut us down. We could not meet the new charitable requirements unless we had a church building, a congregation, and had a constitution. This was not our calling from God. We worked with the churches, but didn't want to be one.

Additionally, the government was moving in a "warm and fuzzy" direction, where one group could not critique another religious group. Tribunals were set up where a person could bring charges against anyone critiquing another's religion, charges of "hate". The government would pay all legal expenses for the one bringing the charges, but not for the one being accused of "hatred". What was happening to our Canada?

CIVIL RIGHTS REMOVED | We watched in disbelief as some Christians and churches who lost their Charity status, were hauled before these tribunals, and ended up losing their homes, savings, and other assets, as they defended their rights of freedom of religion and freedom of speech. I was reminded of tribunals held during the days of the Nazi's. It was surreal.

I was told that if I made public claims that the only way to salvation was through Jesus Christ, and the Bible was the only reliable source of truth, then they would shut us down. They offered to continue our charity status due to our spotless thirty-year record, only if I would teach publicly that salvation was also through Buddha, Hare Krishna, Jehovah's Witnesses, Mormons etc. etc. Other religious books were to be presented as just as good as the Bible, and I was to "keep the enthusiasm out of my voice when talking about Jesus!" The government would require oversight of all our DVD's, to ensure they complied with the new regulations. We were told to shut down our websites immediately.

I countered that we had never said one hateful thing about any other religion. We did give well-researched quotes from these religions, exposing their hatred for any other religion but theirs, but we had never expressed hatred for anyone at any time. Instead, we had worked tirelessly for over thirty years helping any who wished to come free from these oppressive groups. We would not apologize for our stand that true freedom was found in the Person of the Jesus Christ of the Bible. If groups were misrepresenting Christ, we used the Bible to show where they were deceiving their followers. We did not direct people seeking our help to any particular denomination, but only to a relationship with Jesus Christ. This was unacceptable to the Canadian Government.

The writing was on the wall. Before they could terminate our Charity status we voluntarily requested that it be revoked, explaining that we would rather have our integrity to God, than a Government tax number. We were given six months to liquidate the Charity and turn over all proceeds to other registered charities in Canada, or give them to the government under a 100% tax rule. We began the process of shutting down our charity, and after giving both USA and Canadian proceeds to other Canadian Charities, we were officially over in 2008.

During this same time our ministry partners had moved to Nelson, but had not begun any renovations to turn their basement into a ministry facility. We again offered them the opportunity to bow out and close the joint ministry, sell out, take their house profit and relocate. Or, they could retire to Nelson, a beautiful spot to do so, in a house they already owned, in an established vacation paradise.

Additionally, during Mother's prolonged last illness, my Son was left with a three-year old, abandoned by her Mother who had run off to meet a man from another country. She had been having an internet "romance". She had maxed out all my son's credit cards and not paid any rent or bills for three months prior to leaving, to raise funds for her trip. He was devastated, broke, and homeless all at once. I told him to come home and we'd straighten things out when he got here.

CUMULATIVE CRISES | Now we had a multigenerational household. Talk about being in the "sandwich generation". Mother rang her buzzer for me several times a night. By 6 a.m. my granddaughter was clinging to me, suffering from separation anxiety. I did my best to "mother" her and fill the void her own mother had left. One time I took her skating, fell, and broke my knee and my wrist. Now I had a cast and a cumbersome leg brace to add to my difficulties. Our large house was built on three levels and there seemed to be no end to the stairs!

Keith was feeling very tired at this time and I was worn out too. For a total of ten years, I had the daily care of my elderly parents, who lived with us. Mother had passed away in 2006, at age 93, after a lingering battle, with constant pain. One touching experience stands out in my mind. Mother had a final stroke, and the blood clot lodged in her brain in a location that caused her to be extremely agitated. My gentle Mother not only did not know us any longer, but constantly flailed about and had to be restrained. She was in a crowded ward at this time and I could hardly get a chair close to her bed, and I was further encumbered with an arm cast and a leg brace. I prayed that God would find a better place for her to spend her last days.

I was in the elevator the next day and a nurse asked me "Aren't you Lorri MacGregor?" I did not know her. She thanked me for our ministry which had resulted in her family escaping Jehovah's Witnesses through our literature, videos, and teachings. She asked if there was anything I needed. I shared my concerns about Mother. She said, "leave this with me. I am in charge of assigning beds". Because of her, my Mother got to spend her last four days in a private suite with a comfortable sofa bed for my sister and I to use to stay with her around the clock.

Mother's agitation stopped only when I sang the old hymns to her. She would cease struggling and listen. One night in the middle of the night I was singing to her when I felt someone in the room. I turned around to see a nurse standing in the doorway with tears streaming down her face, listening. She was so touched and said it was the most beautiful thing she had seen, and such a display of love. I was so thankful the old hymns had such a good gospel message as not only that nurse, but also my sister and her unsaved family heard those hymns. They would never allow me to share my testimony with them or witness in any way. God made a way for them to hear the old hymns of the church, which contained the gospel message. May the Holy Spirit bring them to Himself.

Mother previously instructed the Pastor that for her funeral she wanted a plea put out to the unsaved family to receive Christ, so we could all spend eternity together. Mother passed away while I was still recovering from my injuries, and the funeral, burial, and many visitors just about finished me off! I was relieved that she was home with the Lord, and not suffering any longer. I still miss her, but look forward to our reunion in heaven.

FATHER | Dad lived on for three more years. He was several years younger than Mom, but decided he wanted to go and be with the Lord at age 93, the same as his beloved Mary.

As his 94th birthday approached, he would not let me make his favorite birthday meal and any plans I tried to make for this birthday would cause him to say "I am going to be with the Lord before I turn 94. He had a final stroke, lingered two more days, and died six hours before he turned 94. I love to picture the two of them together forever. I pray the entire family will be reunited in heaven, as Mother prayed always.

SUCCESSION | Once our partners arrived in 2008, we had major decisions to make regarding the shutting down of the ministry. They wanted to continue on somehow, and Keith and I take full responsibility for not realizing that God had allowed the shutting of the door on our Charity. We should have known that God was saying to us that we had served Him faithfully, but it was time to rest. We too, thought we wanted the outreach to continue.

When someone offers to help and claims God's direction to us, we thought our prayers had been answered. God forgive us. We moved our websites to USA registry, registered as a USA Charity, and set up our ministry as a taxable corporation in Canada. We both used our own funds to buy stock and machinery, from MacGregor Ministries to continue on as MM Outreach, a joint venture.

If it had only been Keith and I we would have just shut down from exhaustion, but we had two willing younger ones to take the load, and they did. They worked very hard. Over time we realized that they could be described as "controlling" and any attempt by us to moderate this behavior resulted in a cycle of anger, then tears, then forgiveness and reconciliation, and then angry, controlling behavior again. We lacked the strength to deal with this destructive cycle and were extremely vulnerable. God forgive us. We, in a discernment ministry, had failed miserably to discern.

At this time Keith and I were undergoing health difficulties. Keith felt very tired and ended up being air-evacuated from Nelson to Vancouver and had four cardiac bypasses during open heart surgery. I was exhausted from flying from Nelson and being at his bedside in Vancouver, and then caring for him, my Father, and my granddaughter at home. Keith did not have an easy recovery, was put in hospital again, and finally recovered from the fluid in his lungs in 2009.

THE PRESENCE | Still, God intervened in a marvelous way during Keith's surgery. We did not know any of the heart specialists at the Coast and had to take whoever was available to do Keith's emergency bypass surgery. On his hospital papers, a name was crossed out and another written in, a new doctor . As one of our sons kept me company in the ICU waiting room the people in the room began to share about each one's surgery, the doctors, etc.

When they got around to me and I said we had just come in from Nelson and named the Doctor who was doing his surgery. There was a collective gasp in the waiting room. They explained how their loved one had been on a waiting list for this particular doctor (who was apparently the best in his field) for two years, and still were assigned another doctor. One family asked me, "who are you that you deserve the best surgeon for your husband?" We are in God's Kingdom, and our Savior had obviously intervened as I prayed earnestly for the best help for Keith. He was released on his birthday and we flew home the next day to continue his recovery. He was hospitalized again for fluid in his lungs, and his coughing was frightening. It was a constant concern for us.

As well, I continued my ongoing struggle as a "sandwich generation" caregiver, trying to be the servant of all to my father, my husband, my traumatized son, and my troubled grandchild. We lacked the strength to be contenders with our ministry partners and did our best to overlook and just "get along". Our spirits were troubled.

We constantly felt reservations about the ministry arrangements, but allowed the new team control, hoping it would all turn out well. It didn't, and we accept the blame for proceeding in the first place, when we shouldn't have. We have asked the Lord's forgiveness for dismissing the warnings we felt in our spirits, and proceeding in the flesh. We tried so hard to go along, but could not, in good conscience submit any longer to their control and treatment of us personally. We decided to resign completely from MM Outreach, and turn everything over to our partners to sink or swim on their own. We wish them well. Sorry it ended so badly, Lord.

In the midst of all this ongoing drama, we still saw God's hand on our lives personally, and know that we serve a great God, with or without an organized ministry. We knew we had not had much time for our older children and wanted to rectify that. All at once, they were no longer scattered far and wide, but we had four out of five of our children now living in the lower mainland of BC. Nelson is our first choice for a place to live, so we decided to get an apartment in the lower mainland and still keep our house in Nelson, and live part-time in both places. That decision was taken out of our hands in December of 2010.

We had ended up buying a large home together with one of our sons and his family, in Langley, BC. We took up residence in the in law suite, and I must admit it was a relief not to climb endless stairs or have to clean a five bedroom, four-bathroom home on three levels!

CRISIS IN 2010 | We had a great Christmas dinner, with sixteen of us around our extra-large dining room table, and we all enjoyed ourselves. I had been coming down with a cold, but other than being stuffed up, felt not too bad. However, the cold worsened and I felt very plugged up. I remembered when I was a constant-cold kid, that my Mom would take a large hankie and make me blow my nose until there was nothing left but air. I decided to try that again. On about the fifth hard blow it felt like someone swung an axe and hit me in the back of the head. I fell forward out of my chair onto the floor with the worst pain I can ever remember.

The last thing I remember as Keith and my son agonized about putting me in the car to emergency in Langley, I gasped "call an ambulance". They did and very quickly I saw the ambulance attendants coming in before I passed out. Keith filled me in on what happened next.

With one quick stop to pick up a head trauma special attendant on the way, our ambulance hit the number one freeway at rush hour. Keith had the ride of his life as the ambulance put on its sirens and flashers and drove at a high speed right down the middle of the white line with cars swerving out of the way. We live in the suburb of Langley, but all head trauma cases go to the Royal Columbian Hospital in New Westminster, about 45 minutes away at the best of traffic conditions. Our ambulance made it through heavy traffic within the 35-minute time frame necessary for head trauma treatment.

I was quickly assessed at the hospital with state of the art technology and was determined to have a number four brain aneurysm (five is the worst). I was stabilized somehow and scheduled for surgery. Keith had phoned the family and they were advised that my prognosis was for brain damage or death. There was one neurosurgeon on staff who had been trained in a procedure called "coiling", but he had left for vacation. He thankfully came back in to do my procedure. A thin platinum thread is passed through an artery in the groin, around the heart and into the left brain. The thread is "coiled" until it forms a loose jumble of threads that slows the bleed and finally stops it. The remaining thread is then retracted. The whole procedure is watched on a screen.

Apparently the other neurosurgeons used the old procedure on the other five head trauma victims admitted at the same time. This consisted of taking out a section of the skull and then clamping off or cauterizing the artery to stop the bleed, and replacing the piece of skull that had been removed. It is invasive and not very successful. With a brain aneurysm such as I had, we were told 30% of people die before the ambulance can get to them, 30% die in emergency before, during, or after surgery, and 40% survive.

Trouble is that the majority of the survivors are left with varying degrees of brain damage. Some are permanently disabled and are housed in a facility. Others go on to lengthy rehab procedures to begin a long process from which they never fully recover. I survived surgery but was in a coma for five days. There was not much hope for me. Our church prayed during this time, and Keith sat with me, bless his heart.

In a coma, I was put in a private room directly across from the nurses' station. Tubes were attached and I was left there, to either wake up, die, or be transported to a long term care facility. After five days in this state, my eyes snapped open and I wondered where I was. I was alone in the room at the time. I remember wondering why there were two big lights side by side on the ceiling for such a small room. I didn't realize that I had double vision, which later cleared up.

I heard a voice, probably answering a phone at the nurses' station across the hall, saying "Royal Columbian Hospital". I puzzled over this as I didn't know the name of the hospital where I had been taken, and the only "Royal Columbian Hospital" I knew of, was one I had passed when we were in Australia, over twenty years before. "What am I doing in Australia again", I wondered. At that moment, a nurse came in and peered at me. She turned on her heel and rushed to the nurses' station, saying, "She's awake! Mrs. MacGregor is awake!" Several nurses rushed in, twice as many as there really were due to my double vision! The head nurse placed her face close to me and said slowly and distinctly, "Do you know where you are?" "I'm in the Royal Columbian Hospital" I replied. There was a collective gasp, as they exited saying "She knows where she is!"

POST-PROGNOSIS | I became aware of all the tubes and lines attached to me and was distressed to find a bladder catheter attached. Years ago I had a stubborn and painful infection from just such a catheter, so I pulled it out. A nurse came in and began exclaiming, "Lord, love a duck, what have you done?" I could hardly speak above a whisper, but I told her I refused to have it put back in. "How are you going to urinate?" she asked me. I pointed at the toilet in my room. "Okay, ducky", she replied, "you get up and go there right now". I found I could not even raise my head off my pillow, let alone get out of bed. I couldn't believe how terribly weak I was. Keith came in and was overjoyed that I was awake. However, I was as white as my sheets and drifted in and out of consciousness and sleeping/waking for the next couple of weeks.

I was told that I could expect "blazing headaches" for about six months. I never had a single headache, but my joints and muscles were very sore from the neck down. As I became more aware of my surroundings and was moved twice to crowded wards, I wondered why I was not being given my thyroid pills and my insulin, which Keith had brought in to the hospital. A scramble ensued and my supplies were found at the back of a drawer at the nurses' station. I had been without them for two weeks. It was no wonder I was feeling so low since I require them daily. I was surprised to find out that they refused to give them to me in any event.

I had also requested an interview with the dietician because all the food given to me since I was able to eat was loaded with sugar. It was Asian cooking (not my favorite) and everything seems to have a sweet sauce over it, and consisted of some variation of high glycemic white rice. I remember being pleasantly surprised one day when some mashed potatoes appeared on my tray with what appeared to be gravy on them. The first mouthful turned out to be sweet hoisin sauce over the potatoes. I spit it out and returned to the yogurt Keith was bringing me. I quickly dropped twenty pounds.

The dietician explained that there was no diabetic food available at the hospital since budget cuts. I could not take my once-daily injection of long lasting Lantus insulin for my type two diabetes, as only type one diabetes insulin was available. They would not give me my own supply, as it was not on the "approved" list. Several times a day I was forced to have my blood sugar taken and type one insulin administered. I was told this would counteract the sugar-laden food, the only kind available. It made me sicker.

The next shock was that I could not have the prescribed thyroid pills I take each day. I had reacted badly to synthroid and so was put on "desiccated thyroid", a natural form of thyroid which agreed with me. I had had no thyroid administered for over two weeks, and then synthroid was forced on me, which made me very ill. My protests fell on deaf ears, as my prescribed thyroid was not on the "approved" list.

My next major hassle was with the high blood pressure medication they were forcing on me. I have an opposite reaction to Ramipril--rather than taking my blood pressure down, it shoots it up. I refused to take it, so in the middle of the night I would wake up to find a spoon with crushed up pills being forced down my throat. The nurses apologized, but had to follow "doctor's orders". My blood pressure climbed to very high levels, extremely dangerous for an aneurysm survivor.

Finally, the day came for my "evaluation". I was given several oral tests, mostly a mix of mathematics, which used addition, subtraction, multiplication and division. I got every answer right. Another test was repeating back a series of unrelated numbers. No problem All right again. The last test was repeating back a series of unrelated words given to me at the beginning of the test, and recalled at the end. I got four out of the five words. I was allowed one hint, and when given that, I got the fifth word. The tester informed me that not even "normal" people scored as high as I did, 100%. I was given a rating of "1", the highest rating for brain aneurysm survivors, and found myself in the top 2% of survivors. Thank you Lord!

The tests determined I had undergone no personality change and really was the same person as before. When God heals, He does a complete job!

By this time, I was able to get out of bed, and push my interveinous rack, to navigate back and forth to the bathroom, and even forced myself to take walks so I could go home sooner. I was still terribly weak, ached all over, and was ill from the medication. I earnestly prayed for help from the debilitating medications forced on me, and finally felt the Holy Spirit prompting me to leave immediately, before they killed me. Weak as I was, I had to fight the establishment to go home. They refused to discharge me, delaying me for another day, and scaring Keith with the threat that I would die if I left, "stroking out".

I had been in hospital for three weeks by now and refused to stay another night. I finally told them I was discharging myself, even though they would not give me my paperwork. I wanted to release the hospital of all liability. My talented but incredibly arrogant neurosurgeon came on the phone and told me bluntly that I would "stroke out" within the week. "So be it," I said, "I'm leaving". A very scared Keith and my daughter-in-law wheeled me out to the car. I was collapsing from the effort to leave and was in sad shape when I got home. I was diagnosed "pre-stroke" at this time. Some head noise remained, but I did not have headaches. Every other part of my body ached, however.

Once home I stopped the Ramipril and my blood pressure came down to my usual "high normal". I got my thyroid function back on track over time, with the pills I could tolerate, and my blood sugar finally returned to normal over time with my proper insulin injection daily, and a healthy diet.

I was so thankful to eat regular food again, like nourishing soup which Keith prepared, and I spent the next three months under the excellent care of our regular doctor, who monitored me closely. I was a flat-out couch potato for three months, mostly sleeping, sometimes unconscious, aching, but so glad to be home. Slowly I became mobile again. Keith took me in the RV to Desert Hot Springs and I spent my days soaking in the healing waters and sleeping but made a good recovery by Spring of 2011.

ADAPTION | How our lives had changed! I was told to be within a half-hour of a major medical facility due to my pre-stroke diagnosis. That ruled out living again in Nelson, so we returned to sell our house. I worked very hard physically, cleaning and loading our RV for our return trip to the Coast in the Fall. We were half-moved already but took two tow trailer loads back and forth to the Coast. Keith had to do renovations to our rental units so I was pretty much on my own with the packing. It was an intense time.

In April we put our house on the market. I still wasn't sure I wanted to give it up, so I really put the Lord to the test! We did not advertise on the internet or the local papers. Instead, we put up a small sign on the front lawn "House For Sale by Owner. No Agents. Phone for appointment". We had the house professionally appraised by the company that appraised for the banks. We fended off all real estate agents.

I (unreasonably) said to the Lord that I would really know it was His will for us to sell if the following conditions were met. 1. The house had to sell at the asking price. 2. There had be no home inspection. 3. The buyers had to be willing to leave us in the house until the Fall. 4. The buyers had to be willing to give our Son and Granddaughter a year to move out and accept their reduced rent until then. 5. They had to buy the furniture we left there.

Confident these conditions could not be met, I knew that I was still emotionally attached to the house. The Real Estate market was slow, so that was okay with me as well. I guess the Lord had other plans, as the house sold in three weeks, and all five conditions were met. Not one cent was spent on commissions or advertising, and we were cashed out and on our way to the West Coast, with our RV packed to the hilt with our final items. We felt so free, not only from the pressures of the ministry, but also from my attachment to the house and Nelson. We thanked God that we had our beach front retreat, and still were able to spend our Summers in our beloved Kootenays. God was with us every step of the way. I was back to feeling "normal" again.

A U-TURN | Since my recovery bordered on the miraculous and unexplained, I agreed to undergo a MRI so my arrogant Neurosurgeon could have another look. It was a decision I came to greatly regret. I traded in my reasonably good health and recovery for several more months of misery.

My concept was that an MRI was much like having an X-ray. I was told that they would have to immobilize my head in a helmet-type apparatus and I was asked if I was claustrophobic. I wasn't. What I didn't know about was the high intensity noise. It was so loud that my ears were ringing, despite thick ear pads. The procedure lasted 40 minutes and was one of the most unpleasant experiences I was ever tortured with. I felt ill and my head was pounding as we went home. I collapsed on the couch and I told Keith I was feeling very much like I did when I first came home after the surgery. Then the pain hit me.

The first nerve pain was the "shingles pain" I endured some years back with a severe case of spinal shingles. I thought I had it again, but we could find no blisters or evidence of it on my skin. Then came a round of polio pain at the back of my knees and down my legs. Nothing else had felt like that since I was 12 years old and had survived polio. What was happening to me? Then the rotor cuff pain hit both my shoulders at once and virtually immobilized me. I had two "frozen" shoulders. I could not comb my hair, dress or undress properly, or get in and out of the bath.

I had gone from recovering enough from the surgery to be able to do hard physical work each day, moving, lifting, and packing. I had walked into the MRI feeling well again, and in one hour was a pathetic, pain-wracked, victim of modern technology. The noises in my head which had continued since the surgery became more intense also. Why had I ever agreed to the MRI?

My General Practitioner called me telling me to come to his office urgently for my MRI results. I was told I had a second aneurysm at the operation site and my life could be over in a heartbeat. While I waited to see the neurosurgeon again on an emergency basis I prepared to die. I tried to remind myself of all the things I had to look forward to in heaven, all the people who had gone on before me to be with the Lord, and especially participating in the great worship scene before the throne in Revelation chapter four. I said my goodbyes to many friends and family.

Finally we came to the neurosurgeon, who had not received my MRI results in his files. He was angry and agitated that he had not been notified. He left us in his office and told me not to move, and he ran from his office to the hospital to see the results on his MRI diagnostic screen. Anxious moments dragged on.

He returned looking puzzled. "Damnedest thing I ever saw" he said. It was not another aneurysm but an encapsulated scar tissue lying below the artery and not blocking blood flow. I was told that the diagnosis for the future was that I was pre-stroke at best, and that should the scar tissue close the artery, it was doubtful that I could survive. Our family has a genetic predisposition to form scar tissue. None of this was in my favor.

The nerve pain I was experiencing was also puzzling, but thought to be "memory pain" triggered by the MRI. It was a case of going to therapy and taking pain killers, and just waiting to see if it would abate after time.

From September to the next February, I struggled with this nerve pain, especially the shoulder pain. I went to therapy but it did not help. Soaking in my hot tub, and lying on the couch with heating pads gave the most relief. The noises in my head lessened somewhat, but my "frozen" shoulders would just not let go. Finally I told Keith I wanted to go to the healing spa waters again near Desert Hot Springs where water came in at a great force, and perhaps my shoulders would let loose. We travelled there in our RV and I spent my time mostly going from the hot water flow, to the couch and back again. By the end of the month I was gaining some mobility and most of the pain was gone.

During these months of pain I was determined that the pain was not going to get the victory over me, but I would not tell many people the distress I was in. I worked to act normally. I went to church and even spoke a time or two and attended the bible studies, and we continued witnessing to Mormons and JW's.

We spent that Summer at our beach lot near Nelson and I did a lot of resting and reading and was able to cope quite well. I was pretty well pain free by the end of that summer, one year of misery ended on a high note, quite humorous actually.

We had hardly walked in the door at home. The phone was ringing. A voice on the other end explained that they wanted to close their file on Mrs. MacGregor. Could I please provide a date of death? After a stunned silence I replied "Speaking!" I refused to return to the hospital for more tests, although I was called in many times.

Chapter Twenty-Two

THE WEST COAST | That winter I faced yet another challenge. We had gone out to dinner, and a snow and rain storm blew in and visibility was bad. Since our friends were coming over after to our house, which is tricky to access, Keith took our lady friend in his car, and I rode with her husband in his large truck so I could navigate. Upon arriving home, I slipped getting out of his high truck and hurt my hip, causing a limp. I couldn't believe I was in pain yet again and confined to the couch.

When my hip was just not getting any less painful, I gave in to pressure to go to an acupuncturist who had helped many people. Needles were put in the length of my leg and hip. Every needle felt like I was being stabbed, and there was quite a bit of bleeding. Nevertheless I endured the treatment, but the noises in my head became very loud during the treatment and did not let up. The ordeal seemed unending. This ended my first and last treatment by acupuncture!

This situation was almost worse than the MRI. The pain lessened but the head noises remained. Finally, as I was sitting in my Hot Tub one night I cried out to the Lord. I know God is Sovereign but I asked Him to 1) Remove the noises so I could function again in the ministry or 2) Just take me home to be with Him or 3) Show me how I could live with this condition and still function in life. I waited to see what the Lord would do.

ANSWER | About two days later I woke up and realized that all the noises in my head were gone! I mean, even the low level noises remaining from my surgery were also gone! There were NO noises at all. What a praise party I had! God is so good! Once again, the doctors who had told me that noises only got worse, never better, and I should have a stent put in my artery to see if that would help, were proven wrong. Praise God!

I went on to teach the Weekly Ladies Bible Study at our church, and sometimes taught at the weekly church study. I know my prognosis is not good from earthly standards, but I will go when the Lord promotes me, and not a moment sooner. Our ministry carried on with visits with JW's and Mormons the Lord brought across our path.

During and after this time of health issues, we experienced several of what I consider "God Moments". They are so encouraging, and show how the Holy Spirit can operate in one's life despite challenges.

SISTER | I have one Sister who has not as yet accepted the Lord. For their fiftieth anniversary they assembled the original wedding party. I had been her bridesmaid and her husband had his friend as best man. So, we had met previously, fifty years before for the first time. This anniversary marked the second time. They had remained friends over the years and my sister and her husband were visiting him some years later at the West Coast. It was a sad visit as he was terminally ill in the hospital and they had come to say goodbye. It was also my 70th birthday and we had a crowd over that Saturday.

Just before my sister left for home, she pulled me into the bedroom and asked me to pray for Ron. She said nothing else had worked, and even though she didn't believe in God or prayer, she knew I did, so would I pray? I said "of course", and did pray for him.

They would see him one last time the next afternoon and then leave. That was a Sunday.

We were at church and looking forward to a long nap when we got home. There was a closing prayer time and so I again prayed for Ron. "Lord, please send someone to him with the gospel message", I prayed. I was jarred when I felt the presence of the Lord and a strong inner voice said plainly, "you go!". I told Keith that as bone tired as we both were, from all the festivities of the day before, we had to drive over an hour and go see Ron in the hospital. Bless Keith, for he never hesitated or questioned me, but said "then we'll go".

The hospital was under construction with a new wing and we had many delays with traffic, and then finally finding his room number, only to find that it was in the other wing which involved a long walk through a lot of construction into another area. As we finally arrived we were told by the nurse that we had just missed his wife and my sister and husband. I believe this was God's perfect timing so we could be alone with Ron.

It was decidedly odd to explain our presence to him. We were barely acquaintances, having met twice in fifty years. I dived right in and said, "We're here to answer any questions you might have about God. We both know you are facing eternity". He said,"I do have so many questions! Is it possible that God would be interested in me now that I am dying, when I haven't had a moment for him in decades? I haven't been in a church since I was forced to go as a child. I refused to go as a teenager, and haven't been since, so how can God want anything to do with me now?"

We could feel the presence of the Lord in the room as God led us to share the story of the workers in the Lord's vineyard, and how those at the very end received the same wages as those who had worked the whole time. (Matthew chapter 20) We explained about grace and God's free gift of salvation. Finally, after more sharing, we asked him if he wanted to pray and receive Jesus Christ as his Savior. Yes!, he said, and we told him we would hear his prayer.

It was the most stunningly beautiful prayer as he asked God for forgiveness for his years of neglect, and truly repented from his heart, and invited Jesus Christ to be his Lord and Savior. His face was beaming as he realized that he was accepted and loved, and would spend eternity with the Lord. The curtain between the beds hid the other occupant but we could hear noises and quiet weeping, and there may just be another soul in heaven, which we will find out in eternity! Had he called out to us we would have gone to talk to him as well, but the Lord knows.

Before we left we prayed over Ron that if it was God's will to raise him up, we would rejoice in his healing, but if not, we would see him for the fourth time in eternity, as our brother in Christ. His wife shared later that when she went in the next morning, she couldn't believe it was the same man. She even thought he might be getting better, and asked the doctor, but was told that, sadly, he tested positive for the deadly infection present in the hospital and would die shortly. He went home to be with his Lord in a peaceful way.

I phoned his wife and told her all that had happened. Although an unbeliever, she went ahead and contacted a Pastor and gave him a beautiful Christian burial. We could not attend as I was speaking at a conference at the same time. She thanked us for going to him, but would not respond to any of our follow-up calls to her in the months that followed. We have left her in the hands of the Lord, with our prayers.

When I phoned my sister to inform her, she was strangely silent through it all, but our prayers continue for the salvation of our whole family. We know as we pray that the Holy Spirit will work in her life to bring her to a decision, and we trust Him.

A BABY | We had gone to a small Langley store to deal with a custom order. The clerk seemed to be very distracted, dropping things, and not able to locate our order on the computer etc. We had dealt there before and she was not like that, so I inquired, "Are you all right?" "No", she said. " My baby granddaughter is in the hospital fighting for her life and the doctors told my daughter to be prepared because things may not turn out well". The baby had a severe case of pneumonia. Tears filled her eyes. I reached out and took both her hands in mine and said, "we need to pray right now!" She bowed her head and we prayed. Other customers came in, so we left to pick up our order a few days later. When we came back I inquired about her granddaughter. Her face lit up as she shared that the same day we had prayed, later in that day the baby had started to breathe on her own again and improved so rapidly that she could be taken home that same night!

Customers came in and so we left with our order. About a week later we made a special trip to see her. We didn't know if she was a believer, or where she stood in her spiritual life. She shared that she was a Christian and had a home church already. We have been blessed so often to bring Christ to bear in people's tragic circumstances.

THE SMOKER | One time Keith and I had been out to dinner and it was pouring rain. Keith offered to go and get the car, so I was left huddled under a small roof overhang with a man puffing on a cigarette. I remarked that it was pretty miserable for him to have to be out in this weather just to have a smoke. "Have you ever tried to quit?", I asked. He shared that he had tried everything to quit, programs, patches, etc. I asked him if he had ever tried asking the Lord for help. He said, "what do you mean?" I shared that often when we cannot do things in our own strength, the Lord can help us. I could see Keith driving from the far end of the parking lot so I knew I had to be quick. I said "Just pray to Jesus Christ, tell him how you have struggled, and ask him to come into your life and heart, be your Savior. Ask Him for help to overcome your smoking problem. Read the book of John first in the Bible and find a good church. We like Calvary Chapel by the bridge". As I left, he said, "I will, and thank you!"

DEPARTURE PLANS AND NEW ARRIVALS | Keith and I finally got down to the unpleasant task of arranging our funerals. With our blended family, we did not want any unpleasantness over arrangements, should the Lord call one or both of us home. We called a local funeral home and booked an appointment with a lady representative. While going through the arrangements, she asked what we had done before retirement. We replied that we had spent thirty years in the full time ministry. "What kind of ministry?", she asked. I responded that I had been a Jehovah's Witness for fifteen years, and had dedicated my life to teaching Christians how to present the gospel to those deceived in the cults.

Her eyes got big and round and she pointed at me and exclaimed, "I think you are the answer to my prayers!" She shared how she had been in bondage to a cult and had escaped some twenty years before. However, every time she tried to go to a church, all the warnings against the church from the cult rose up and made her too uncomfortable to continue. She longed to have a close walk with God, but needed the residue from the cult's doctrine cleared up for her. She had prayed that God direct her to some Christian who could help her. Talk about timing!

I had spent two years researching and writing the script for a DVD about her cult, and was in a good position to help her. In fact, knowing people in the ministry, there were about two people in the Province who could have helped her, and I was one! So, God took two procrastinators about funeral arrangements and put them with a person who worked only two days a week in the area. This is a work in progress, but we know God is on the move in her life. We left her with a DVD that answered her questions.

MISSION FIELD AT YOUR DOOR | We have had many experiences over the years meeting in people's homes who also invite the Jehovah's Witnesses or Mormons. They learn how to witness to this missionary field walking up to their doors, and we are always blessed. One time we drove quite a distance to be there for two Mormon missionaries who had an appointment with a Christian. They did not show up. I even asked the Lord why He had us come all that way when He knew driving after dark was not easy for us.

Soon, our householder's father came home from work. The son shared how his dad was cynical about his Christianity, and would probably go to his room. After supper the father remarked that the Jehovah's Witnesses had "finished him off as far as religion was concerned". He added, "I am finished with God". As he prepared to walk off I said, "Yes, but is God finished with you?" He hesitated long enough for me to share that I had been a JW for fifteen years, and I, too, was so finished with religion, but not with God. He sat back down and we were off to the races, so to speak.

For hours, we shared memories of past conventions and "new light", and reversals on doctrine, and how JW's were truly a manmade organization and false prophets by biblical definition. I shared how much Christ meant to me now, and we promised to meet again, this time at our house, when we can all have a free evening at the same time! This, too, is a "work in progress" and we are excited to see what the Lord will do.

THE PROBLEM OF SUCCESSION | Recently there have been a few "sentimental journeys. Keith and I travelled in our RV and said our goodbyes to many ministries who have been part of our lives over the years. We were surprised to learn that many had tried to turn their ministries over to other folks, even their children, but all these ministries were struggling. We had all enjoyed the blessings of the Lord while we were in charge, and had to agree that none of us were in the will of the Lord when we tried to pass our calling on to others. Still, we are all serving the Lord in personal ministry, as best we can, without officially being a charity.

FAMILY | Another sentimental journey for my sister and myself was to a memorial service for our Mother's last remaining brother, Uncle Louis. There we met with our childhood playmates, our cousins. We knew our cousin Blaine, living on the family homestead, was soon to die so we got to say our last goodbyes to him, one of the few Christians in our family. Our cousins are good people, mostly living by good standards, and are honest and reliable, but without Christ, except for one, maybe two. I prayed for God to make an opportunity to share the gospel, but with such a crowd, and all talking at once, there never was a good opportunity.

Finally one night, after a busy family dinner, the last of the crowd left at 11 p.m. As we were saying goodnight to the two cousins where we were staying, the one closest to me growing up suddenly asked me to tell them about how I met Keith and about our life together. I had never been able to share with my opposing sister the exciting testimony surrounding our meeting and life together. She shut me down for almost forty years when I would try to share with her. Could this be the time? Yes!

I breathed a prayer and began. My two cousins and my sister listened attentively for over two hours. The younger cousin hugged me after and thanked me. My sister and other cousin and I went off to bed. I was so excited that I was still awake at 4 a.m. praising God! The next day we went off to the cemetery to visit the family graves. I had often wondered about my cousin Roger who had died tragically some decades before. He was a long haul truck driver and always came to visit me over the years I was a JW.

Imagine my delight to see his tombstone with the Christian quotes on it. He died safe in the arms of Jesus. I'll see him again! Also many deceased family members I never knew had Christian gravestones as well so I'll get to meet them someday!

My Mom and Dad and I had tried to share with Uncle Louis but he was resistant. We continued to pray for him over the years. At his memorial a retired minister shared how he and Louis had had endless discussions while they worked in the workshop at the retirement home. He didn't elaborate, but it was a comfort to me to know God had honored our prayers and put the gospel message before him prior to his death. I'm hoping there was a blessed reunion in heaven with him and my parents.

My sister and I, now the matriarchs of the family, continue to have companionship and a growing closeness, as I continue to pray for her and her unsaved family. We visit every year. Her eldest daughter, while not professing Christianity, said the example I set in caring for my Mom and Dad inspired her to care for her own parents in the same loving way.

BLUE MOUNTAIN | Another sentimental journey was to the "Witnesses Now for Jesus" Conference in 2014. What a reunion it was, as we embraced our friends and ministry partners after many years away. One main speaker was unable to come, so I was offered his place on the program and given a chance to share God's goodness. What a joy! What an incredible love fest! We pray God gives us the health and strength to go again to Pennsylvania.

TERRORIST | On our prior flight to the Conference, I was teaching on "Understanding Armageddon" and had my notes in my carry-on bag. One security person saw my file. "Armageddon" must be a buzz word used by terrorists. I was pulled out of line, had my bag examined, and got extra pat-downs. They even made me take down my upswept hairdo to make sure I had no weapons in it! It was an embarrassment as my hair is waist-length and I made quite a spectacle with my messy hair and my jumbled bag and had to pull myself together while Keith and others had a good laugh at my expense!

Our usual plan of booking a window seat and an aisle seat on our flights, so we could share with whoever the Lord put in the middle seat, didn't work. We had so many interesting times of sharing on our many flights over the years, but this time the middle-seat person plugged in earphones and kept their eyes on their electronic gadget the whole time. Since then, the same thing seems to happen repeatedly, so we sadly retire this opportunity to share our wonderful Lord. It was good while it lasted!

CUBA | Our adult children are always in our prayers and we try to respond to every invitation they give us so we can spend time with them. Our daughter recently invited us to join them in Cuba where they have time to relax before opening their BC wilderness Lodge for the busy season. We hoped we could stand up to the rigors of the trip so we booked to go.

I had been having increasingly painful episodes of diverticulitis, the condition which killed my grandmother at age 77 and took the life of my mother at 93. Often sitting is very painful, so the long plane ride and airport layovers were not easy on me, but I persevered. Cuba has an excellent reputation for health care and even sells insurance at the airport to cover all medical expenses at a very low cost, so I felt I would be okay, even if I had to go to hospital. Thankfully, after a rest, I was able to enjoy our week with them at the Casa, and even took Salsa lessons!

The last night before the flight home, I decided to eat very lightly, so ordered a salad at the restaurant. Unfortunately it had been prepared using the local water to wash the leaves, and I became ill in the night with a swollen, tender abdomen. and intestinal upset. A 1956 Buick taxi took us on the two hour ride to the airport. The road had not been repaired since the 1959 revolution, and the car seemed to have no shocks to cushion the bumps. There was also no speedometer working, no seat belts, but the radio blared loud Salsa music. By the time we arrived at the airport, I knew I was in big trouble.

I have a high pain threshold from years of practice dealing with pain, so we soldiered on. We had a four-hour layover in Toronto and I tried to stretch out and take some of the pressure off. We took off at 10 p.m. for Vancouver. Thankfully, we had business class seats, so had slightly more room than usual. Upon arriving in Vancouver, the discomfort increased. Leaving the plane, I headed for the nearest washroom. When I got up I was surprised to find much bright red blood left behind. This had never happened before and I was really frightened. I knew a diverticulitis bleed would lead to immediate surgery if it did not stop. We made it to the car park and then the hour drive home to Langley. The bleed had by this time become a hemorrhage. I felt like my life was draining out of me. Later testing showed volume loss, a drop in iron, and dehydration. My blood pressure dropped 50 points. By this time my son Randy was involved and he and Keith insisted I go immediately to the Emergency room.

GREY CUP | I knew I did not have the strength to sit in an emergency room as I desperately needed to lay down and sleep first. We had been up all night. This was Tuesday, Keith's birthday, and Randy and I had tickets for the Grey Cup game on Saturday. I had been looking forward to this all year, and didn't want to miss it. So, I asked Keith and Randy to lay hands on me and pray with me one last time, and if I was still bleeding afterwards I would go to the hospital.

When we prayed I didn't ask God for a healing, but instead asked Him to stop the bleeding so I would have a few days to recover and attend the Grey Cup game. I was ashamed of my "frivolous" prayer but also knew that God sometimes allows us the desires of our hearts. After prayer I felt like another rush of blood was coming on and saw instead two large blood clots. The bleeding stopped and has not returned to date.

I thankfully collapsed into bed and recovered over the next few days enough to go to the game. Our ride to the game fell through, so we had to travel the hour it would take by sky train. We drove to Surrey and boarded the train. It was crowded, and people were standing, but unbelievably there were two seats left vacant. I dived into them and was able to sit all the way to the game. We had a great time there, despite me being weak. Afterwards, Randy warned me that never did they have seats for the ride home. We were able to buy our return tickets at a special booth at the game only because we could produce exact change. At the last minute before leaving the house I had put a handful of change into my pocket and that bought our return tickets! This saved us from huge lineups at the ticket machines at the station.

We arrived at the boarding platform along with a huge crowd of fans. Although there were people already standing I spied a single seat at the very back and was able to sink into it. Randy later got a seat. We arrived back at home. Randy remarked that I seemed to live a blessed life and it was fun going out with me to see what God would do. I even have a nice memento, a picture arm in arm with Canada's Prime Minister, Stephen Harper, who was seated close to us.

COUSIN | My large unsaved family are always in my prayers. Recently a cousin phoned me for the first time ever. The whole family was in turmoil as their son in university had presented them with an announcement that he was now a baptized Mormon at age 18. Could we come over and talk to them? I prayed earnestly for the Lord's help, as there was no point in taking my Bible and reading Scriptures. What to do? I shared my testimony of what had happened to me at age 18 when I was vulnerable and seeking for God. They all listened closely. My testimony of my born-again experience was included, of course. We have left these dear folks in the hands of the Holy Spirit, and pray for the salvation of the whole household. We left a helpful DVD behind. We heard via another cousin that they appreciated our visit.

BLOOD PRESSURE PROBLEMS | In the summer of 2015 my blood pressure began reading in the 170's over 65, with my usual pulse rate of 90. We were relaxing at our Lake Lot near Nelson, BC. My usual reading most of my life was 150 over 65, with a pulse of 90. "High normal" was the best reading I could manage. Since my diagnosis was "pre-stroke" and I was a brain aneurysm survivor and I had type two diabetes I was at very high risk. We went to a walk-in clinic and my nightmare with blood pressure drugs began. The doctors tried every kind of blood pressure medication known, but my pressure kept rising, and I had several bad reactions, including opposite reactions (higher, not lower). We arrived home to Langley, and the round of specialists began. Alternate drugs were tried, with no positive results and bad reactions. At one time I was taking 15 pills a day to no avail.

Finally, the heart specialist threw up his hands in frustration and wrote a letter to the experts at the University of British Columbia to see if they would take my case. My symptoms were sufficiently "weird" and my diagnoses of "Pre-stroke" and "Severe, resistant Hypertension" got me accepted. After a four-month wait my appointment was set. By this time, I made the decision to wean myself off all medication. This was against all medical advice but my readings were no different, with or without the drugs. Now my BP readings were spiking at over 200 systolic, and the diastolic readings had risen to near 100. "Normal" was defined at 120 over 80.

I was thoroughly examined at the UBC Hospital by the best specialist in the Province. At the end he said "I have a diagnosis". The night before, exhausted from praying daily for a healing, I asked the Lord to please give me a correct diagnosis. The doctors who had seen me previously had done their best, but I just didn't fit with anything they knew.

I held my breath to hear my results.

First off, I was told that my diagnosis of "Pre-stroke" was in error. I had lived with this for six years, thinking that I could be gone in a heartbeat, and severely limiting my travel plans. I felt like the weight of the world lifted off me. Then, he continued, the "severe, resistant hypertension" was also wrong. What I had was called "isolated systolic hypertension", a rare, much less severe condition, and possibly genetic. Yes, I am not healed from hypertension, but now I know what I have, and will do my best to manage the condition. One small, inexpensive pill per day seems to agree with me. People with this (probably genetic) condition can live long and productive lives. I could breathe again!

The doctor was not finished. I had been diagnosed with type 2 diabetes based on one blood test of 7.2 some fifteen years ago, with no other diabetic symptoms. The tingling I sometimes felt in my feet was not diabetes-related. I controlled my blood sugar for ten years by diet, but finally had to resort to insulin injections to keep my blood sugar readings in line. He informed me that he did not believe I had type two diabetes at all, and my daily use of insulin may have harmed my body's ability to make its own insulin.

Presently, I am weaning myself off insulin to see if my body will again make insulin on its own. Whatever the outcome, it can be treated. I felt like I floated out of that hospital. Thank you, Lord.

So, this brings us up to date. I enjoy teaching the Bible Study each week, and thank God for the wonderful women who attend. We all truly love and care for each other and bear one another's burdens and share our joys. Keith continues on with his internet discussions about the Lord and we help out with counseling others.

We thank God that he has used our story to minister to those who have had a divorce and remarriage and are struggling with disapproval by some Christians and the church.

He gave us a fruitful and satisfying ministry despite these prejudices, and we are so privileged to minister to others and share our relationship with our wonderful "God of the second chance". His great and total forgiveness is available to us all. We thank God for our closeness to our children. It is our hearts' desire to spend eternity with them, but we cannot violate their free will. We pray they will want to live forever with us and turn their hearts to Jesus in the future. We are grateful that two of them have made that decision already. God knows. I thank God that Keith came into my life some forty years ago. Because he shared his faith with me, five generations of my family have now come to Christ. My grandmother, her son my Father, and my Mother, myself, and my two children and their children.

Keith and I always joke in the mornings and say "Well, we woke up on the right side of the grass this morning!" We thank God for all the good years we have shared, and always thank Him for what He had done and will yet do. To God be the Glory!

CONCLUSION | Have I lived up to my name? I think so. Truly I have battled back like a warrior when life tried to take me down. I am ever conscious of the help of the Holy Spirit and God's presence in all circumstances. There has never been a dull moment for Keith and I. We look back on shootings, helicopter crashes, rebellious children, blended family joys, doctrinal disputes, church splits, revivals, blessings, renewals, acknowledgments, faithful friends and fellow warriors, radio and television appearances, video productions, Satanists, witches, and, in the end, great personal contentment. Absolutely *IMPOSSIBLE...* It had to be told.

Addendum:

MY ORIGINAL POEMS | During our long ministry, I took a break from heavy research and writing to remember my sense of humor over the years. I have been encouraged to include some of these efforts in this book.

Jehovah's Witnesses teach that Jesus Christ is an Archangel named Michael, "a god", in heaven, only a man on earth, recreated at his death to be Michael again. My questioning of this doctrine was the first step out of the Watchtower. To honor that, I composed this short poem:

THE WATCHTOWER JESUS

The Watchtower Archangel Michael shows
an alarming trend to recycle.

In the heavens, "a god", then Jesus the man,
dissolved, recreated as Michael.

JW's will tell you today, that THEY are the truth
and the way,

but their Christ is an Angel, their dates are a tangle,
They are told what to do and to say.

My Jesus, no angel is He! Shed His blood
on Calvary for me.

He is God, He is Man, I, with Him take my stand,
No need to recycle Michael!

———

I couldn't believe the Mormons actually believe this doctrine on God, so I wrote a poem, summing it all up:

OF MORMON GODS

There once was a man from Kolob,
Who, because he lived his life so good,
"a god" he became, Elohim was his name
The council of gods made earth his domain.

This heavenly father of flesh and bone,
was not content to just sit on his throne.
Many wives had he, busy as a bee,
producing "spirit children" for eternity.

Two kids of his quarreled over who would be Lord,
Jesus and Lucifer were they.
One was redeemer, and one was the devil.
A strange brotherhood I'd say.

Elohim looked on down, and a virgin he found,
but he didn't leave her that way!
A child she produced, named him Jesus the Lord.
He married three times, so he wouldn't be bored.
This isn't the Jesus of Scripture, Who for my salvation did die.
So, Mormons, I'm sorry, I won't see you in glory,
Joseph Smith has told you a lie!

———

I had a milestone birthday celebration for Keith when he turned seventy, and wanted to write him a special poem:

"MY TRIBUTE TO KEITH ON HIS 70TH BIRTHDAY"

I always remember the first time we met.
I wanted no men in my life, but yet...
You patiently waited and bided your time.
You proved as a man you were so fine.
You looked at me with your eyes of blue.
You promised to love me and always be true.
You helped me move to my Nelson home.
You let me know I was never alone.

You even took my two boys in stride,
And loved them too, as I was your bride.
We set up shop in our home on the Lake.
Adjustments came, with give and take.

Although unexpected, our family grew.
Children were five, and not just two.
Attilla our dog, Pussywillow our cat,
The MacGregor home was where its at!

We worked together side by side,
Building our business and our lives.
We nurtured our kids, supported each other.
We formed a strong bond, step father, step mother.

It wasn't all easy, but we trusted the Lord.
The ministry meant we would never be bored.
We moved to the Coast to Fraserview,
Next, to Tsawwassen with the whole crew.

We weathered the troubled teenage years.
We held on to our love to conquer our fears.

The kids all turned out to be just fine.
We toasted our freedom with a glass of wine.

We've travelled much of the world around,
With adventures and trials we did abound.
We returned to Nelson to retire,
In our hearts still burns the fire.

And so, my love, hats off to you,
A quarter century and we've stayed true.
So raise a glass and join with me,
In a toast to my Keith at Seventy!

———

Here is an old effort I found which I wrote for my Parents' Fiftieth
Wedding Anniversary when many relatives joined us in Balfour, detailing
their lives together for the first 50 years:

FIFTY YEARS TOGETHER, Bill and Mary Robison

Let me tell you the story of my Mom and Dad
Two of the nicest parents a girl ever had.

My Mother was born on the Saskatchewan prairie.
Her trip to the mountains was really scary.
Over curves and hills the Greyhound proceeded,
For as a housemaid her services were needed.

Some brothers were already in residence here,
In a shack by the Lake, so they would be near.
I wonder if they remember the time, with but only one pot,
One made tea, one made coffee. At least it was hot!
This curious mix was served with the phrase,
Coffee or Tea? Which will it be?
All received the strange contents you see!

Meantime, up on Houston Street, a young mountain man
felt a strange new force, and said,
"There might be more to life than my dog and my horse."
Having brilliantly deducted this fact,
He set about making up for this lack.

Not just anyone would do for him.
She had to cook, clean, and cater to every whim.
Horse and dog were deserted, and with a gleam in his eye,
He spied this fair country maid, nervous and shy.

"She's the one!" he cried, as he looked in her eyes,
and dispensed with both their dates.
From that moment on, an item they were.
It was not too long till he married her.
His horse and his dog got one last fling,
A prospecting trip to buy her a ring.

Poor Mother had to cross the mountains again,
But was allowed a stop in Saskatchewan,
On their way to an Island in Ontarioland,
to live with his relatives on the Manitoulin.
Dad reported to a war camp in the North
To run their office, traveling back and forth.

Mother had quite a time coping, you see
with the local vocabulary.
Lilacs were laylocks, and on the side of the stove
there reposed a "resiboiler", by jove,
which heated the water, and outside the door,
There hung ducks by their necks,
till they dropped on the floor.

At that time they were "ready to eat"
Mother longed to beat a hasty retreat!

Nevertheless, true love prevailed,
The depression was ending,
and a new future hailed.

This time in their travels they would not be alone,
for two gorgeous daughters now graced their home.
For many years we moved to different locations.
Mother made us a home in all destinations.

Father labored long and hard, and so the years went by.
Still there was time for hunting and numerous fish fries.
I know just how inept I was at learning how to cast.
I caught trees, rocks, the seat of my pants.. finally fish at last!

I also caught my sister, who had little patience with me,
and beat me about my body, with great regularity.
Mom and Dad endured our fights, which dragged on for years,
until we were diverted by boys...that brought them
new fears!
For years they patiently waited to use their telephone.
At last we presented them with "Empty Nest Syndrome".

My Sister was determined that they should
grandparents be,
and in rapid succession presented them with three.
I could not be outdone, so I had two rather quickly.
But she carried on, ahead of me, with yet another three!
I countered with three stepchildren,
and took the lead you see,
For I now have two grandchildren, to none upon her knee!
This friendly feuding is a joke, I hope for your enjoyment.
The grandchildren are all grown up,
most even have employment!

We are a diverse bunch these days--
we live both near and far.

We've all come the miles to say how
special they both are.
We thank you all for coming, through all types of weather,
So Mom and Dad can celebrate fifty years together!

(Note: Since this time, my sister has 8 grandchildren. I also have 8
grandchildren, plus six great-grandchildren.

———

ODE TO THE LAST GENERATION -

This epic poem is just too long to include in this book. I was invited to
speak at the Conference of "Witnesses Now for Jesus" at Blue Mountain
Retreat in Pennsylvania. The JW's were forced to redefine the word
"generation" as we were long past the generation of 1914, that was supposed
to see Armageddon. I decided to present a history of the Watchtower
Society in verse! Quite an undertaking, but well received. If anyone wants
an email copy please request one at **kgmacgregor@gmail.com**.

———

Here is a treasured poem written for me some years ago by my elder son,
Robert:

FOR MY MOM

In her, I see the strength that sustains my soul.
In her, I find courage to strive for my goal.
In her, I recognize myself, both good and bad.
In her, I discovered the best friend I've ever had.

From her came my zest for life and love,
From her the will to rise above.
From her, a heart strong and true.
From her, a vision fresh and new.

From her I get my sarcastic wit,
From her, my patience, a little bit.
From her, my sense of right and wrong.
From her, my voice to raise in song.

With her I can be nonsensical or sane.
With her, life can be a serious game.
With her, each day is a brand new start.
With her, my hopes find a sheltering heart.

To her, I am her copy, her clone,
To her my heart is always known.
To her, who taught me how to live,
To her, who showed me" live" equals "give."
For her, I go the extra mile.
For her I try to share my smile.
For her I always do my best.
For her, I stand out from the rest!

Love, Robert

————

Looking back, I see how blessed my life and legacy has been. Keith and I have celebrated our 40th wedding anniversary, so I wrote this poem:

Forty Years Together

It's October 4, 2015--and here's where we have been.
We made our vows before God and man
On the date Armageddon "began".
Oops! Another false Watchtower Prophecy!
We mark it each year, currently reaching 40!

We built us a home on Kootenay Lake,
Keith surprised us with three more kids to take.

Our private "Brady Bunch" had history to make.
Our blended family has survived, mostly by God's grace.

Becoming a taxi service to town grew old fast.
After two years we knew it could not last.
We renovated Lorri's house in town
So our children could readily move around.

God was moving too, as He used us daily to serve.
Lorri taught the Bible. Keith headed up the
Full Gospel Business Men's move.
Many came to serve the Lord and a church
was built and grew
Bernice Gerard heard Lorri teach and
brought us to Fraserview.

We joined the ministry team and helped
to pioneer Sunday Line,
Which included the gospel to the cults on radio and TV.
Soon we guested on national and international shows
And were launched into full time ministry.

Our launch involved a robbery in Phoenix, Arizona
Where Lorri was shot and miraculously saved.
The story went international, and instead of the grave,
We shared the experience with people we hoped to save.

Our thirty-year ministry took us far, to five countries
and a new media plan.
We returned to the Nelson area to set up our
base, and worked in our printshop,
Producing videos, audios, and thousands of booklets,
and magazines, all non-stop.
We renoed our house to take our parents in and
our family additionally grew by two
To four generations under our roof--

No kidding, we were pooped!

Exhaustion and death tried to claim us with Keith's
heart attack,
Add my thyroid problems, diabetes, and broken bones,
of troubles we had no lack.
Caregivers to the "sandwich generation", we prayed
for someone to have our back.

We endured betrayals from trusted ones when they promised help to give,
We grew in grace through it all, and
God's peace never left us.
The many friends and fruits of our service
Gladdened our hearts and sustained our purpose.

We missed our older children, so retired to the Coast.
Four out of our five children now live real close.
Robert looks after family business, as our legacy grows by eight
grandchildren, and six great grandchildren!
(Maybe more--who knows?!)

Soon after moving, Lorri had a brain aneurysm
and nearly died,
But God stepped in and gave her back her life and ours.
Calvary Chapel surrounded us with love and prayer.
And we enjoy our church home, and our dear friends there.

We look back on forty years of married love
For each other, our children and God's love from above.
It's been so good to have lived this life,
With each other, and God ever present.
We look forward to more years on earth together,
However long they may be.

Thank you God for these 40 years -- Now on to eternity!

Other Materials:

BOOKS BY LORRI:

Coping With the Cults:
What You Need to Know about Jehovah's Witnesses

BOOKLETS BY LORRI:
(Published by MacGregor Ministries)

Answers For the Cults
A Look at the RLDS
Blatant Blunders of the Watchtower Society
Brighter Light? (Changing Light in the JW's)
Counterfeit Christianity - How To Identify A Cult .
Christadelphians And Christianity
Concerns About the Promise Keepers
Christian Counterfeiters
Could Jesus Be a god?
Drifting Into Deception
Examining Seventh-day Adventism
Examining The New Age Movement
Examining the JW Publication, "Should You Believe in the Trinity?
Fractured Families
Facts SDAs won't Tell you.
How Reliable is The Kingdom Interlinear Translation?
Is The Trinity True?
Is Comunal Living for Christians?
Jehovah's Witnesses And The Real Jesus
Jehovah's Witnesses And The Question of Blood Transfusions
Mormonism, Is It Christian?
Questioning the Worldwide Church of God
Reviewing the Vineyard
Should you pay Attention to "Pay Attention to the Book of Daniel"?
The State of the Dead
The Witness At Your Door
The Pagan Roots Of Jehovah's Witnesses

The Baha'i Faith And Christianity
The Church Controversy -Women!
Viewing the Vineyard
We Are The Prophets Of God

DVDs (SCRIPTS WRITTEN OR CO-WRITTEN & RESEARCHED BY LORRI)

Drifting into Deception
Jehovah's Witnesses and the Real Jesus
The Witness at Your Door
The Witness Goes Out (sequel)
Jehovah's Witnesses- A Non-Prophet Organization
Batttling Over the Children (JW Custody Cases)
Seventh Day Adventism, The Spirit Behind the Church
The Trinity, Eternity Past to Eternity Future
Faulty Fads in the Church
The Perils of the Prophets
Word Faith--Is it the Word, or the Faith of the Bible?

ABOVE ITEMS MAY BE AVAILABLE AT:
MMOUTREACHINC.COM